PAC
?/01

P9-DHN-552

# Creative
# Selling

# Creative Selling

DAVE DONELSON

Entrepreneur Press
2445 McCabe Way, Irvine, CA 92614

**Managing Editor:** Marla Markman
**Book Design:** Sylvia H. Lee
**Copy Editor:** Peter Kooiman
**Proofreader:** Megan Reilly
**Cover Design:** Amy Moore, Mark Kozak
**Indexer:** Ken Della Penta
**Production Designers:** Mia H. Ko, Marlene Natal

©2000 by Entrepreneur Media Inc.

All rights reserved.

Reproduction or translation of any part of this work beyond that permitted by Section 107 or 108 of the 1976 United States Copyright Act without permission of the copyright owner is unlawful. Requests for permission or further information should be addressed to the Business Products Division, Entrepreneur Media Inc.

This publication is designed to provide accurate and authoritative information in regard to the subject matter covered. It is sold with the understanding that the publisher is not engaged in rendering legal, accounting or other professional services. If legal advice or other expert assistance is required, the services of a competent professional person should be sought.

Library Of Congress Cataloging-in-Publication Data

Donelson, Dave.
    Creative selling: boost your b2b sales/by Dave Donelson.
    p.cm.
    ISBN 1-891984-15-2
    1. Selling I. Title.
HF5438.25.D66 2000
658.85--dc21

00-030669
Printed in Canada

09 08 07 06 05 04 03 02 01 00                    10 9 8 7 6 5 4 3 2 1

*For Nora, who not only puts up with it all but makes me more creative, too.*

# TABLE OF CONTENTS

# INTRODUCTION

hy did I write this book and why should you read it? The answer to the first part of the question is simple. I wrote this book because I've enjoyed a long and successful career in sales and can help you do the same.

But why should you read it? Because it's about a proven, systematic way to become a better seller. The Creative Selling System not only earns you more money, it turns your sales job into an enjoyable, satisfying experience.

When you practice creative selling, you gain control over your own success. Good salespeople seize every opportunity that comes along. *Great* salespeople don't wait—they create opportunities for themselves. That's what creative selling is about.

What would your commission check look like if you added just one more sale to your weekly total? What if that one sale was to a customer who became the source of sales for years to come? One additional sale per week doesn't sound like much, but if you do it every week for a year, the cumulative effect on your income is astounding.

All you have to do is follow the step-by-step instructions in this book. I broke the creative selling process down into steps that are easily learned and practiced. Each step logically follows the one before it, leading you down the path to a successful sale. Stay on the path, take one step at a time, and you'll make more sales.

I developed the Creative Selling System through trial and error. By using different sales techniques on my own prospects and accounts, I determined which ones worked the best. I later observed the salespeople I hired, trained, and managed using these techniques, confirming my beliefs about creative selling. Finally, I dissected this proven sales method and turned it into a step-by-step sales training program—the Creative Selling System.

This book isn't about theory—it's about action. It's a how-to book that shows you the steps to a successful sales career and gives some alternative strategies to use along the way. There are a couple of ways you can use this book.

First of all, learn by doing. Read a chapter and apply its techniques when you sell to your customers. If you take about a week to absorb and practice each chapter, you'll better understand the process and use it more effectively. Participants in my training programs are required to use each step with a real prospect before I go on to the next one. It takes a little more time, but the results are spectacular.

You can also use this book as a source for problem solving. For example, if you're having trouble with closing a particular customer, review the eight closing techniques in Chapter 10 and pick one that you haven't used yet. If you feel like you're in a professional rut, check out Chapter 13 for exercises that boost your enthusiasm.

No matter what you do, don't just read about creative selling. Do it! Unleash your creative sales power. You'll make more sales and have a lot more fun.

# CHAPTER 1

# THE MICHELANGELO OF SALES

**M**ost of us don't associate the word "creative" with "selling." For some, the word "creative" conjures up images of starving artists dressed in black "trying to make a statement" with paint and old auto parts. Creative people wear berets and read *The Village Voice*. Salespeople wear ties and read *The Wall Street Journal*.

At least these are the popular stereotypes. But don't salespeople create things, too—like opportunity? Don't salespeople create demand for products and services? Customer satisfaction? Wealth? Most salespeople certainly create wealth—for themselves, their companies and their customers.

The nature of the sales process is, in fact, creative. A good salesperson creates demand where it doesn't exist. He or she creates a message (the sales pitch) using various media (face-to-face calls, telephone calls, written presentations, slide shows) that influence an audience (the prospect). A salesperson explores new territories (cold-calls), introduces new ways of thinking (persuades prospects) and makes the world a better place (provides customer satisfaction).

OK, maybe I'm overstating the case a bit. Lots of perfectly productive salespeople are nothing more than harvesters of existing business— they take orders, fill out paperwork, collect their commissions and go home. They never break rules, and they hate new products that disrupt their orderly natures. New customers are a pain in their behinds. "Don't bother me with creativity," they say. "I'm too busy selling."

These salespeople still play a role in our economy, even though they're well along the road to extinction by order-processing technology. But I'm here to talk about creative selling, the favorite activity of wild, vibrant, risk-taking sales fanatics—the Michelangelos of sales.

These people practice creative selling whether they know it or not. They use the power of ideas to create customer satisfaction and wealth.

# THE CREATIVE SELLING SYSTEM

I've had the immense pleasure of studying, practicing and teaching creative selling for many years. I've worked closely with, managed, and observed thousands of salespeople—some creative, some not. This experience helped me develop the Creative Selling System. Creative selling unleashes your idea power—your ability to make more sales and create more personal wealth by selling ideas instead of products. That's what this book is about.

The "system" in the Creative Selling System is the part of my approach that makes it work. A system is nothing more than the repeated application of proven techniques to accomplish a desired end. My system applies selling creatively to the goal of producing more sales.

The Creative Selling System is a framework that enables you to be a more effective, efficient salesperson. When you work within that framework, you apply creative techniques to every step of the selling process, from prospecting new accounts to servicing old ones. You use your personal creative talents (and we all have them) to solve problems and create opportunities for your customers.

You're probably going to find that you already use many of these techniques. You wouldn't be studying this material if you weren't already a creative salesperson—or at least didn't suspect that underneath that beige tweed order-processing exterior lurked a sales fanatic waiting to break loose. What you should expect to get from this material is the ability to recognize these methods when you use them, to understand why they work for you, and to learn how to use them more frequently and effectively.

We begin with the basic assumption that you are a pretty effective communicator. You know your product or service and are interested in professional growth, job satisfaction and better customer service. You wouldn't mind making more money, either. These are pretty safe assumptions.

We also assume you are willing to invest your time, money and effort into achieving these goals. Nothing good happens without effort, especially in sales. Learning how to use the Creative Selling System is the same. If you're not willing to invest the time and effort to practice, you'll never reap the rewards. If that's you, stop reading and go do something you really want to do. Life's too short.

If you're still with me, that's a good sign. It means you have an open mind—the single most important component of creativity.

## Creating New Business

I'm going to explain the Creative Selling System almost entirely in the context of selling a new account. My focus is on developing new business—not because existing accounts aren't important, but because the same techniques you use to sell new accounts work even better on the ones you already have.

When you sell business-to-business (B2B), you have to constantly work on new accounts because your old ones are never 100 percent secure. Their plans change. Their business changes. Their customers change their habits. Their competitors "zig," causing your customer to "zag." Every change in your customers' business has the potential to change their relationship with you and their need for your products and services.

Your competitors are nibbling on your existing customers, too.

### HOW TO BE A HOME RUN HITTER

Think of using this material the way a good baseball player uses batting practice. Concentrate on the positives of swinging smoothly—doing the right thing over and over—until it becomes automatic. Follow the creative selling steps again and again until they become second nature. You'll be pleasantly surprised at the home runs you hit with new business and satisfied customers.

Contradicting what you say, bringing in new products, even—horror of horrors—undercutting your prices! Even the smallest competitor hurts you by taking away an account here and there, and a big one can devastate your sales and income.

If you're not constantly working on bringing in new accounts, your sales and commissions are going to wither away—sooner than you think. In some industries, customer loyalty is so tenuous that 40 percent of accounts turn over each year. These companies have to replace nearly half their account base every year just to stay even.

In most companies, there's another reason salespeople should be developing new business: it's their job. Almost every sales job description includes the direct or implied function of introducing new users to the company's products. If the orders just came in, there wouldn't be any need for salespeople, just an order-processing department. You should think of new business development as job insurance.

The main reason you should work on new accounts is that it's *fun*—the risks and challenges are tremendous. There are few thrills in life that match the exhilaration of closing a new account.

Why? You do it yourself. You have some help, of course—from your boss and the other departments in your company—but ultimately, you make sales happen and that's the fun part.

## Creative Selling Principles

Now, let's get down to business. I adhere to three creative selling principles:

1. Focus on the largest potential accounts.
2. Know the customer's business.
3. Sell ideas.

The first principle is pretty obvious. If you only sell the biggest accounts, you'll sell more and work less. It's much easier said than done. This step requires immense discipline and taxes creativity.

Before you can effectively sell prospects, you must know their respective businesses. Sure, if you make enough calls, you can stumble across a few people who need your product, but you're just filling the order they were waiting to give you. To identify potential needs and inform your prospects of them (one of the primary goals of creative selling), you have to know the prospects and their respective businesses.

The third principle is that you must sell ideas instead of products. Ideas uncover new opportunities, anticipate potential problems and provide solutions for your prospects. Selling ideas instead of products means you have to present your "products" in the context of the prospects' needs. You can't just lay out a list of reasons for them to buy your deal.

This is consultive selling with a bang. Consultive sellers ask the prospect what they want and then give it to them. Creative sellers do a whole lot more.

In creative selling, you uncover needs that prospects may not

## ENGINEERING A SALE

My friend Matt is both a salesperson and an engineer—a very unusual combination! Matt had a prospect who was responsible for the public structures owned by a county government, everything from playground equipment to bridges.

Matt specializes in the structural analysis of communications towers. This prospect sent out a request for proposals (RFP) for inspection of the county's communications towers, which are used for two-way radios and other communication systems.

Matt looked beyond the RFP at the entire assortment of structures his prospect managed. Instead of just submitting a proposal for the towers, Matt also pointed out that the county bridges were subject to the same stresses (weather, materials deterioration, etc.) as the towers. These stresses were potentially dangerous, so Matt proposed an inspection of the bridges using the same rigorous professional methods his firm applied to the towers.

This wasn't covered in the RFP, but Matt made the sale by *creating* an opportunity to study a potential problem that hadn't existed in the prospect's mind. He then *created* a solution to the need by designing a service that his firm didn't normally provide (bridge engineering). My friend's mind was open to the possibilities and he used creative selling techniques to create an opportunity.

realize they have, and provide creative solutions to those needs, even if you have to adapt your product to do so. In consultive selling, you're limited by what the prospect tells you. In creative selling, you're limited only by your own imagination.

Creativity is a limitless resource with limitless possibilities. You'll always succeed if prospects rely on you as a source of new ideas. Remember, one sale won't make you rich. *The Pieta* didn't make Michelangelo rich or famous. His entire body of work—the statue of *David*, the design of St. Peter's, the ceiling of the Sistine chapel—branded him a superstar. In the same way, salespeople must keep pitching new ideas if they hope to build an ever-growing income.

## Creative Selling Advantages

There are many advantages to using the Creative Selling System. It's not product-driven or even market-driven. It goes beyond that to become a market driver itself. The company that consistently practices creative selling widens its market by creating new opportunities in the undiscovered needs of its customers. Creative sellers don't respond to the needs of the marketplace—they create new ones.

And what does that do to the competition? They're out of the race before they even know it has begun. How can they compete to satisfy a need even the customer doesn't know exists? The competition is forced to play a continual game of "catch-up" and "me-too" in response to the sales that the creative seller is making.

The creative seller builds something else of immense value: a strong relationship with the customer. When the prospect realizes that you're there to talk about their needs (not about your need to sell something), they're much more open to listening to your proposal. When they see the amount of *your* time invested in *their* success, they'll be willing to hear you through completely. And when they discover that you're also bringing them an idea to use—giving them something of value before they give you any money—their ears will open even wider.

This relationship will build on itself, creating a bond between the buyer and seller based on the seller's ever-increasing value to the buyer. The creative seller gets easier access to decision-makers, moves earlier into the decision-making process, and is seen not as an adversary but as an ally. The creative seller becomes the idea resource for the customer. The buyer turns to the seller not for more products but for more ideas on how to enhance his business.

Ideas are scarce. They don't exist until someone creates them. They can be copied, but only after the original hits the market. Since there's nothing to compare it to, the price of an original idea is determined solely by perceived value to the buyer. There is no competitive bidding or price shaving for market share—just the seller's ability to create perceived value by persuasively presenting the idea as a solution to the buyer's needs.

There are also some great tactical advantages to selling ideas. One of my favorites is that the prospect can reject them. That's right, the ease with which the customer can say no is actually an advantage to idea selling. Let me explain.

Traditional sellers walk into a prospect's office with a presentation listing reasons to buy their product. They present their case with arguments and evidence, much like a lawyer does in a courtroom. They listen to the opposing case (objections from the prospect) and rebut them. The whole process is about winning a debate with the prospect.

> Creative sellers don't respond to the needs of the marketplace—they create new ones.

There are basically three people involved in a court of law: the judge, who hands down a decision, and the plaintiff and defendant, who each present arguments. In the court of sales, however, the "judge" also happens to be the opposing attorney. Your chance of getting a fair trial is pretty slim. One reason closing ratios are typically so low for many salespeople is that they try to rebut the judge!

But losing the case—or getting a "no" from the prospect—isn't the toughest part. It's the fact that once this judge hands down the decision, it's pretty final. There's really no appeals process in sales—it's pretty hard to get back into the courtroom with the same old case. Since you gave all your best reasons to buy during the first presentation, you're likely to hear "I've heard this one before," when you come back the second time. You have to offer something new to get back in the door.

When you sell ideas, you've always got a reason for the prospect to see you again. Your new ideas will keep their doors open. You're

> ## THE THREE COMMANDMENTS
>
> 1. Thou shalt focus on thy largest customers.
> 2. Thou shalt know thy customer's business like thine own.
> 3. Thou shalt sell ideas.

not coming back to make the same old pitch, you're offering something new.

Of course, part of your presentation includes the reasons your product will satisfy the prospect's needs. You *do* need to make your arguments. If you structure your presentation the way I suggest, the prospect focuses on the desirability of your idea, not on the reasons for buying your product or service. Your "arguments" will go unanswered and you can present them again, along with new ideas.

Another tactical advantage to selling ideas is how the prospect responds to them. Traditional sellers make presentations full of information about their own products or services. So what do prospects talk about? The *seller's* products, of course.

But when you talk about ideas unique to your prospects, they'll talk about how the idea applies to *their* business. This is all you want—to hear prospects talk about their needs, concerns, and objectives. The more they talk about their needs, the better you'll be able to shape your ideas to meet them. It's a powerful feedback loop that works in your favor.

# CREATIVE CUSTOMER RELATIONSHIPS

I've found in years of working with clients in hundreds of different lines of business that they all want and need ideas. I've yet to meet a businessperson that's truly not interested in hearing an idea that will make them more money or solve a problem. They'll present plenty of obstacles, of course, but most business managers and owners are willing to hear—and buy—ideas on improving their companies.

When you become identified as "the idea seller," prospects will keep their doors open for you—seeing you before they see the dozens of non-creative salespeople clamoring for their attention.

The more ideas you present to prospects, the more feedback you'll get. The more you learn about their businesses, the more needs and opportunities you'll see, which in turn leads to even better ideas. The stronger your ideas, the better they work for customers which, of course, leads to more satisfied customers. Satisfied customers are repeat customers—the most profitable customers of all.

The Creative Selling System isn't a get-rich-quick formula. I don't wave any magic wands or offer any secret potions to entice your prospects. But the Creative Selling System is foolproof. Anyone can use it by following the steps I've outlined.

Creative selling isn't the exclusive domain of a few wild fanatics. You don't have to know about brushes and paints to be creative. Anyone with a set of ears and eyes connected to an open mind can become a creative seller. All you need is the desire to learn, the willingness to try new things and the personal motivation to practice them until they work for you.

Are you ready, Michelangelo?

# CHAPTER 2

# START
# CREATING

W hat's the first step in creative selling? Coming up with a creative idea, right? Wrong! It's investigating prospects and uncovering needs they might have. Secondly, you set specific goals for them—then you create an idea. Ideas are third—needs come first.

## SELLING ON THE FIRST CALL

One of the concepts I've been preaching and practicing for years is also one that is often the most misunderstood. I believe that you should present a specific idea-based proposal to every prospect on your very first call. This suggestion invariably sends the consultive sellers into convulsions: "How can you make a proposal without ascertaining the need?—Won't the prospect think you're arrogant?—What if your proposal is wrong?"

If you follow my method, making a proposal on the first call won't seem brazen. For starters, your first call on prospects shouldn't be your first communication. In addition, you should do a needs analysis before the call. In fact, the time and effort you put into needs analysis will dwarf that of a typical consultive seller who goes into the first call with a questionnaire. Your needs analysis will be more accurate, which means a more accurately targeted proposal.

The consultive selling approach begins with a needs analysis call, in which you ask prospects about themselves, so you can give them a good proposal on the second call. There's certainly nothing wrong with the intentions of that approach, but in my experience, it seldom works out the way it's supposed to. There are several reasons.

## The Truth About Consultive Selling

For one thing, few prospects answer your questions unless they are already interested in your product. Pre-qualifying prospects this way may be a good time management method, but "not interested" prospects could be valuable sources of new business. Their numbers are growing every day because the needs analysis approach is hugely overworked. More and more prospects refuse to invest their time in it.

Prospects are bombarded with offers to study their financial needs, manufacturing systems, advertising plans, and insurance programs. They've become immune to the it's-a-valuable-study-with-no-obligation-to-buy pitch. In many industries, the same prospect submits to multiple consultive analyses with the same company because the vendor has such high turnover in its sales force. In turn, fewer and fewer prospects are falling for the "needs analysis" gambit.

But what about prospects who *do* answer your questions? In general, I don't believe they give you the most accurate information on which to base a proposal. They wouldn't see you unless they had some preconceived notion of what they wanted to buy. This tends to color their answers—not that the prospect would lie to you, but when someone already knows the answer, they often interpret a question to fit it. Their interpretation of your question may lead to confusion over the answer—assuming they're fully cooperative to begin with.

What are some things you want to learn when conducting a needs analysis? Most analyses boil down to two questions: "How can the prospect best use my product" and "How much money can they spend on it?" Variations on the first question may get some fairly accurate answers, but the second question often generates purposefully wrong answers. Most people are pretty sensitive about giving out financial information to strangers.

## Every Sales Call Is A Transaction

That's what you are, after all—a stranger. This is the first call—you don't know them and they don't know you. All they know is that

## CONSULTIVE TIME WASTER

A client of mine who owns a Texas furniture store told me how her local newspaper advertising department once did a needs analysis for her store. She regularly advertised the store in the paper, but the rep told her they could do an even better job if their team spent some time studying the situation. Sounds good, doesn't it?

The newspaper's team consisted of the ad sales rep, the retail ad sales manager, a layout artist, and two other people whose functions were never completely clear. Their "study" consisted of the ad manager asking a series of questions like, "Who's your target customer?" and "When are your busiest months?" While he and the sales rep asked questions, the other three team members wandered around the store. After all the questions were asked and the answers written down, the team left, promising a report within a week.

This needs analysis interview took up two hours of my client's time. The "report" she got back was a proposal for doubling her space contract for the next year. She never did find out what the people wandering around the store were doing.

The point of the story isn't that this needs analysis process was handled poorly, it's that this is a fairly typical *perception* most of your prospects have of the process. They've either had this happen to them or know someone who has, and they will probably resist when you want the time to conduct your needs analysis "study."

you're there to get something (information and time) and that they get something in return (a proposal). View every sales call as a transaction in which valuable items change hands. Even if a sale doesn't occur, information changes hands—and that's valuable. In a solid transaction, items of equal value are exchanged in a two-way process. On the consultive sell first call, however, the prospect gets nothing of value in return for his or her time and cooperation.

In the Creative Selling System first call, the seller "pays" for the prospect's time with an idea—and ideas are valuable.

What you get for your payment is information about the prospect. That information comes in the form of responses to your proposal—not as answers for your questionnaire. Since the responses are spontaneous and voluntary, they're generally more accurate than answers to questions. For the same reasons, the prospect will often give you a greater amount of information because they're not limited by the specific subject of your question.

## Prospect Priorities

If you're in business-to-business sales, you know where you and your product generally rank on the list of priorities of most prospects. It's usually way down there near the bottom of the list simply because business operators or managers have so many situations clamoring for their attention every day.

Start with personnel (the biggest headache of all) and all the issues that go with it: hiring, firing, motivating, compensating, absenteeism, benefits, training, and on and on. Evaluate the cost of

### TO TELL THE TRUTH

People seldom lie when they're telling you something on their own initiative. They want you to have the information, so why falsify it?

When you request the information, though, it's another story. They basically have three options: 1) Tell the truth, 2) lie, or 3) refuse to answer.

The problem is that it's hard to determine what's true and what's not. For example, if you ask prospects how much they budget for a specific expense, like advertising, they might tell you $200,000 (assuming they don't tell you it's none of your business). But how do you know $200,000 is correct? Maybe they're understating in order to get you to lower your prices. Maybe they're overstating because they're including the onetime cost of permanent store signage or the lost-revenue expense of promotional discounts. The point is, you don't know.

But, if you make a proposal of $100,000 for ad space in your magazine and the prospect tells you $100,000 is half the company's annual media spending, you can be pretty sure $200,000 is an accurate figure.

goods if the business is a retail establishment, or the cost of materials if it's a manufacturer. These contribute directly to the profit margins, which are thin and getting thinner in most businesses today. Consider the "infrastructure" of the business—overhead items like rent, utilities, computer systems, debt service, and insurance. Take into account partners and shareholders, not to mention the most important thing of all—customers. And don't ever forget that old bugaboo: taxes, in all their myriad forms.

With all these matters weighing on the prospect's mind, is it any wonder that it's tough to get an appointment—especially one to ask a bunch of questions?

It's even tougher when you factor in the competition—other salespeople. And I'm not just talking about your direct competitors. I'm referring to the army of salespeople peddling items and services that deal with all the above issues. Vendors, manufacturer's reps, insurance agents—the list is endless. They all want a few minutes of the prospect's time every day. If the prospect saw them all, he'd never get anything else done. If you want an appointment, you have to break through the clutter. You should pay the prospect for his time, not expect him to pay you.

# TRUE NEEDS ANALYSIS

OK, you get the message: Make an idea-based proposal on the first call. But back to the question at hand: How do you come up with an idea without doing a needs analysis? You don't, of course. What the creative seller does is invest some time and energy into research about the prospect's potential needs using every available resource except a first call questionnaire. I suggest that you ask yourself a series of questions about the prospect and see if you can get the answers from any of the many available sources. Believe it or not, you can even pretty accurately estimate the size of potential orders for your product or service without directly asking the prospect. And you can do it in advance, making your first call proposal seem perfectly reasonable.

## Research The Prospect

I like to build a file for each prospect that contains everything I can find that pertains to their business. That file doesn't only have to contain items related to your product or service. It should cover anything you can find about the prospect's business, market and customers. It should be very wide in scope because you never know where an idea is going to come from. And the information should always be gathered as if you were the prospect himself. You want to know what the prospect wants to know. Ideally, you'll learn to think like him.

> You want to know what the prospect wants to know. Ideally, you'll learn to think like him.

Use a little library and/or online research and a little common sense and you'll be able to answer your questions pretty accurately. If you want to know the dollar volume of the prospect's market, for example, visit the U.S. Census Bureau. They publish the census of retail trade, wholesale trade, manufacturing, and agriculture with data gathered every five years. It's available by SIC code, broken down into county and three-digit ZIP code cells, which give you a pretty accurate estimate of the prospect's market size. It's a good starting place and it's free.

If you want to know how many locations the prospect operates in, or how many competitors there are, check the Yellow Pages. Once again, the information is readily available and there's no cost to you.

Then take a little drive around the market, checking out the relative size of the prospect's and competitors' locations. Count the number of cars in the parking lots. Take a tour if they offer one. If your prospect is a retailer, stroll through the store and note the number of employees. Which of your competitors' products are on the shelves? Which of their delivery trucks are parked outside the loading dock? You don't have to be 100 percent accurate, but you'll be surprised at how much information you gather just by keeping your eyes and ears open.

Regardless of the type of business the prospect operates, ultimately they sell something to someone. While you're out and about, observe the prospect's customers, since that is the next area of general research. Find out who their customers are, why they buy this type of product or service, and what steps they take in the decision-making process: How long is the buying cycle? What alternative options do they have? Why do they buy from this particular business?

Once again, securing this information is mostly a matter of time and common sense. Check the trade publications for the prospect's industry for data on their customers and their preferences. Look at general sources such as *American Demographics* magazine and others with similar information. When appropriate, do a little "mother-in-law" research. Informally survey friends and relatives about their impressions of your prospects and your prospects' competitors. Look at your prospects' advertising. Who are they trying to reach? What appeals are they making?

## Think Like Your Prospects

Even if your information isn't directly related to the product or service you're selling, it's important information to prospects. It's the kind of information they use as a basis for their purchasing decisions. You'll use this information in a number of ways, particularly in pre-qualifying the prospect. You'll also use it to conduct what I call a "one-person brainstorm," which is the process of translating the information you've gained into a set of goals. The prospect achieves these goals through the purchase of the idea you present.

This background data gathering may seem like a lot of directionless, time-killing work. It's not. It's as much a part of the creative process as putting brush to canvas. The information you gather will be just as (if not more) accurate as that gained from the consultive selling first call.

# ESTIMATING PROSPECT POTENTIAL

Let's now take some of that information and talk about methods for estimating the size of a prospect's potential account. I'll discuss the dangers of estimating too high or too low, and I'll point out several ways to use the estimates you develop.

Let's answer that burning first question: "Why estimate when I can just ask the prospect?" First of all, you should estimate new prospects' potential spending *before* you call on them for the first time. This forces you to do some research into the account before you make the first contact—which in turn makes that first call more effective. Taking this step helps you identify some of the client's potential needs and helps you spot opportunities for selling your product or service.

Secondly, most new prospects don't want to talk about their money with someone they've never met—and if they do give you a figure, it may not be accurate—accidentally, or on purpose.

## Potential Vs. Budget

It doesn't matter how much money the client *currently* spends—it's how much they could *potentially* spend. Many businesses significantly under-spend in certain product and service categories. This is due in large part to salespeople who concentrate on getting their share of the status quo, rather than on creating new dollars. In my experience, if you give a client a good reason to spend more, they will. That's why you should estimate their *potential* spending—not just their current budget.

Estimating the potential gives you a target to aim for—something tangible that serves as a compelling reason for you to invest your time in this client. The estimate will help you shape the scope of your proposal in terms of both total dollars and value. An accurate, well-founded estimate also gives you a starting point for future negotiations.

What happens if your estimate is wrong? After all, you're really just preparing an educated guess—and guesses can be off the mark. Let's look at the two possibilities: estimates that are too low and those that are too high.

## Estimating Too Low

If you estimate too low, you might leave some money on the table. Your competitors have a chance to lay their hands on it, and that's obviously not good. But there are some other, not-so-obvious dangers to estimating too low. You may also inadvertently insult the prospect by bringing her a proposal that's beneath her consideration. You'd be surprised at how often this happens. Or you try to pitch the top decision maker only to discover that your proposal is so small that it gets delegated to a subordinate.

When you believe the client doesn't have much potential, you also tend to price your product lower than its true value to make it more affordable. A combination of these factors leads to the biggest problem with underestimating: when what you sell and what they get is simply too little. Don't estimate too low—you're not playing it safe; you're just playing it cheap.

## Estimating Too High

How about estimating too high? Are there any dangers there? Yes, but fewer than you might think. There is always the outside possibility that your proposal is so big, it scares the prospect away. This happens so rarely, it's really not a consideration. The biggest danger of estimating too high is that you spend too much time on a client who doesn't warrant it—a time management problem that's quickly and easily corrected once you make your first call.

One of the biggest "sell-in" problems I face when coaching salespeople is the widespread fear of pitching a proposal that's too high. I remember Jerry, an advertising salesperson from Michigan, who just couldn't believe that any of his prospects could spend more than $10,000 annually—the maximum amount he would ever propose. His prediction became a self-fulfilling prophecy.

> Don't estimate too low—you're not playing it safe; you're just playing it cheap.

In my training programs, I usually work with the salesperson on specific prospective accounts. Jerry targeted a local dairy for this work. I didn't know much about the prospect, so I did some quick and dirty research. Jerry and I walked through a few of the grocery stores in town and checked the dairy cases, where we saw that his prospect had about half of the facings. I guesstimated the dollar volume of the dairy's products based on the number of stores in the market, the wholesale value of the product, and its volume per store.

This process gave us a potential advertising budget for the dairy of $60,000 annually. When I told Jerry that he should make a proposal for that amount, he turned pale and staggered as though he were going to faint.

"He'll kill me," Jerry said. "I couldn't ask him for that much money. He'll think I'm a crook." Since Jerry didn't believe that this (or any) prospect could spend more than $10,000, he thought he would be talking them into something that wasn't financially healthy.

"Our estimate might be off, but not by much," I said. "Besides, what do we have to lose?"

Against his better judgment, Jerry put together an idea-based proposal for $60,000. Since he was afraid to make the presentation by himself, I went with him—but only as an observer. Jerry made a good presentation until he got to the point where he was supposed to ask for the $60,000. He froze and couldn't say anything.

The dairy owner looked at the amount of money on the page and did some quick calculating. Jerry was ready to duck and run. Finally, the prospect spoke.

"This is about what I spend on *all* my advertising and promotion, Jerry," he said. "I'm not really comfortable putting all my eggs in one basket, which is what I'd be doing if I bought your plan. Could I schedule your ads every other week? Would that cut my costs in half?"

Jerry was still paralyzed, so I answered with a resounding, "Yes!" I thanked the dairy owner for his business, took Jerry by the arm, and led him to the car. He had just made a sale three times larger than any he had previously closed. Jerry became a believer in the worth of estimating a prospect's potential *before* making the first proposal.

## Estimating Methods

The best way to avoid the dangers of estimating too high or too low, of course, is to first prepare an accurate estimate. There are several methods you can use. I recommend that you try two or more and then compare the results to improve your accuracy. Most methods center on first estimating the prospect's gross sales, then applying an expense-to-sales ratio to determine the spending potential.

So how do you estimate the prospect's gross annual sales? You can use several sources. One of my favorites is the U.S. Census Bureau. Every five years, the Census Bureau conducts a census of retail trade and one of service industries, as well as the census of agriculture, wholesale trade, manufacturing, etc. You can get data from the most recent census at your public library or from the Census Bureau's Web site (www.census.gov). The data available includes annual sales, number of establishments, and number of employees for hundreds of business categories. What's more, it's available for every county in the United States—so you can retrieve the actual sales for your prospect's market within a five-year time frame.

Let's look at an example of some Census of Retail Trade data and use it to prepare an estimate using three different methods. Assume your prospect is a retail garden shop with one location. According to the Census of Retail Trade in the county selected, there are 14 retail nurseries and lawn and garden shops with collective annual sales of $10,660,000. As a group, they have 76 employees.

Given these three figures, you can estimate your prospect's sales three different ways. First, you can make an educated guess as to their market share based on the size of their store relative to the other stores in the county. If your survey leads you to believe that the prospect garners a 20 percent share of the market, their annual sales would be a little more than $2 million.

$10,660,000 x 20% = $2,132,000

Another method would be to calculate the average sales in this category, which simply means dividing the sales by the number of stores. This method yields an average annual sales figure of $761,000. You then adjust that figure up or down, again depending on whether the prospect's store is larger or smaller than the others in the market. If your view of the 14 competitors' stores shows that the prospect's location is 50 percent bigger than the average, you would estimate their sales at slightly more than $1 million ($761,000 plus 50 percent equals $1,141,500).

$10,660,000/14 = $761,000

$761,000 + 50% = $1,141,500

The third method is to calculate the sales per employee ($10,660,000 divided by 76), then multiply it by the number of employees in the prospect's store. In this example, that works out to $140,000 per employee in the category. If your prospect has 20 full-time employees—or their equivalent in part-timers—you would estimate annual sales of $2,805,000.

$10,660,000/76 = $140,000

$140,000 x 20 = $2,805,000

If you're dealing with a multiple store prospect, don't forget to adjust your figures by multiplying the per-location estimate by the number of outlets. And I'm sure you've noticed that each method requires you to be familiar with the prospect's store—and the competitions'. Some reconnaissance before you make that first proposal is always a good idea. In fact, you can't make an accurate estimate without it!

These three methods yielded a range of estimated annual sales from $1,141,000 to $2,805,000. Averaging the three numbers gives you a pretty safe bet of $2,026,000.

$$\begin{array}{r} \$2,132,000 \\ 1,141,500 \\ 2,805,000 \\ \hline \$6,078,500 \end{array}$$

$6,078,500/3$ estimates = $2,026,00

Remember, you're not trying to land a human on Mars, here. You're just trying to determine the size of the ballpark your prospect plays in. You want to come up with an estimate of their spending potential that they will be comfortable talking about.

Once you've estimated the sales, use one of the readily available compilations of expense-to-sales ratios to calculate the prospect's potential budget. There are several studies available at most public libraries or from various trade associations such as the National Auto Dealers' Association. They will break down expense categories for types of businesses—sometimes for geographic regions—and calculate the ratios you need. They'll tell you things like the average retail garden shop spends 4.3 percent of its annual sales on advertising and promotion. Or that liability insurance costs for a widget manufacturer are 1.5 percent of gross sales. If you don't have such a source for your particular product or service category, do some rough calculations yourself using information you know about your current accounts.

You can use other sources to estimate a prospect's annual sales as well. *Sales and Marketing Management's Data Service* (also available from the library or from the publisher, *Sales and Marketing Management*) is a great tool for this purpose. *American Demographics* magazine regularly publishes consumer spending data for many product categories. There is also a wealth of online information. Of particular interest is the Small Business Administration's Web site (www.sba. gov), which is full of information about all sorts of businesses.

## Using The Estimate

How do you use your estimate of the prospect's potential? First, shape your proposal. The estimate of total potential spending gives you a sense of the dollars you can go for, the value of the components you can build into your plan, and even the length of contract to propose. You should also use the estimate to allocate your time to the prospect.

I can't stress how important it is to make a specific proposal on your first call on the client. Investing time into researching the prospect makes a great first impression. Plus, the information gained in response to your proposal will help meet the client's needs on subsequent calls. You'll also be surprised at how often the prospect's response to your proposal confirms your estimate of their spending potential.

Preparing an estimate of the prospect's potential spending pays off in the long run. You work smarter, not harder, when you take the time to estimate how much the prospect is worth, before making the first call.

# SETTING PROSPECT GOALS

But what about the idea part? How do you know if the client can use your product or service without calling on them first? Invest a few minutes in a one-person brainstorm. Organize the information you've gathered about your prospects' businesses—who their customers are, what areas they serve, what the competition's like—into a series of about six subjects. As an example, here are the questions I ask when preparing a marketing proposal:

○ Who is their best customer?

○ What is the frequency of the best customer's buying cycle?

## A SIMPLE CAUTION

One major point to keep in mind: Don't go through your estimating methodology with the prospect! Your estimate simply prepares you for the initial call. It's not going to get you an order. Focus your presentation on the benefits of your idea—not on how you came up with the dollar amount. Remember, the prospect is buying your proposal, not your methodology.

○ How complex is the buying decision?

○ Does the best customer have alternative sources for need satisfaction?

○ What is the market position of the prospect and each of the top three competitors?

○ What apparent special problems does the prospect face?

In this example, the service you are selling deals with the marketing of their business. Your product may involve a step in the manufacturing process or a service that involves back office operations. Whatever your field, you can draw up a list of five or six typical subjects applicable to your product or service that are pertinent to almost all prospects!

## Brainstorming Step 1

In the Creative Selling System, you're going to answer these questions yourself—as best you can—using the information gathered during your reconnaissance visits and research. You're also going to apply a great deal of common sense and a little "mother-in-law research." Let's work through these questions for your garden supply store prospect:

○ **Who is their best customer?** Note that you're looking for their best customer, not their average one. As you know, the 80/20 rule is highly accurate in most businesses. You're interested in the 20 percent of the customer base who provide 80 percent of the sales. In your example, the best customer is a homeowner, since apartment dwellers and renters seldom spend a lot on landscaping. A slight majority of those customers are women. (This assumption may not be politically correct, but if you stand in a garden supply store for any length of time, you'll probably find that it's true.) She is probably a physically active person who enjoys the outdoors—attributes dictated by the type of product being sold. Since she's also a homeowner, she's probably over 30, since that's when most Americans buy their first home.

○ **What is the frequency of the buying cycle?** Again, common sense tells you that the nature of the products sold means heavy buying in the spring (with maybe weekly store visits) and a tapering off in the heat of the summer. There is probably also a slight increase in store traffic in the fall, when bulbs and trees are traditionally planted. Even the best customer doesn't spend much at the garden store in January. Although this is common sense, you might want to verify it by visiting a garden and nursery Web site.

○ **How complex is the buying decision?** Are customers going to spend a lot of time making complex decisions (Which car do I buy?), or make spur-of-the-moment decisions (Where do I get gasoline?) Your garden store's best customer is probably a picky customer who shops around for quality, selection, and price (probably in that order), but makes plenty of point of sale purchases. If you're not a gardener, ask friends and relatives how and where they shop for garden supplies. This is what I call "mother-in-law" research and the answers will be accurate enough for your purposes.

○ **Does the customer have other sources for need satisfaction?** Mail order, whether generated by a catalog or Web site, is another way customers get what they want and need—and so is shopping at a discount store, many of which carry garden lines. Check ads in your local paper for this information.

○ **What are the market positions of the prospect and the top three direct competitors?** I won't go through a lengthy explanation of the full theory of positioning here. Just suffice it to say that each competitor in a category occupies one marketing position in each consumer's mind. Positions are those qualities that influence the consumer's decision to choose one brand or store over another to satisfy a particular need. They are the consumer's perceptions of factors like price, selection, quality of merchandise, service, convenience, etc. Different factors are more or less important to different consumers, but the best customers I'm talking about will generally put the same weight on one outstanding factor.

In the case of your garden shop, that one factor will probably be quality of merchandise, since the serious gardener knows that cheap plants are often inferior stock. Ask a gardening expert about your prospect. In this exercise, let's assume you hear that your prospect is the low-price leader in the category, with top competitors occupying the selection, service, and quality positions.

O **What apparent special problems or advantages does the prospect have?** Location? Parking? Employee turnover? Has the business changed hands recently? This list can be endless but the basic question deals with factors that might influence the best customer's purchasing decision that aren't covered by the previous five questions. This is the "miscellaneous" category.

## Brainstorming Step 2

Now take the second step in your one-person brainstorming session: Identify a need. Go back and take a look at the answers to each of the six questions and ask yourself: Does this information indicate a possible need or goal for the prospect that is related to my product? You'll want to write down one goal for each question, which gives you six when you're finished.

Once again, let's continue with the garden shop example. Remember, you're selling a marketing program, so the goals you list will relate to that type of sale.

> You seldom try to change consumer behavior, but a goal might be to get the jump on the competition.

O **Best customer:** If the prospect's best customer is a physically active female homeowner, one goal for the prospect's marketing plan would be to expand the market by attracting the husbands of those women. They may not be the decision makers, but they will be what I call a "decision influencer." If you can provide some sort of incentive for them to visit the prospect's garden shop, they'll likely bring their wives.

O **Buying cycle:** Peak season is spring. You seldom try to change consumer behavior, but a goal might be to get the jump on the competition. Bring the best customers into the store during February and March—they are more likely to return in April and May.

O **Buying decision complexity:** The best customer will shop several stores in search of the highest quality plants and seeds, so a goal for your prospect is to get on every best customer's list. The best customer probably won't go to all 14 different stores. Make sure your prospect's store isn't ignored.

○ **Alternative need satisfaction:** Your prospect's best customer may spend a sizable portion of her gardening budget on mail order suppliers. One goal might be to attract mail order customers to your prospect's store.

○ **Competitive positioning:** Your analysis tells you that your prospect's store owns the low-price niche in the market—but the best customer is primarily concerned with quality. One goal of your marketing proposal might be to raise the perceived quality of your prospect's merchandise.

○ **Miscellaneous factors:** Let's assume that your prospect's store is the most conveniently located. A goal for your marketing program might be to exploit this advantage and create more store traffic.

## Using The Brainstorming Results

Now you have a list of six possible goals that the marketing service you're selling to the prospect can accomplish. Note how the six goals you've outlined are not necessarily related to each other. In fact, they could be mutually exclusive. This is brainstorming, where each thought is put on the table and then explored on its own merits.

You'll also notice that these are pretty specific goals. The less generic they are, the stronger the statement they make. Try to avoid buzzwords and general benefits like "increase store traffic" or "slice manufacturing costs" when you're framing your goals. Try to make the goals more specific as in "increase store traffic from senior customers on Tuesdays" or "slice the 32-ounce widget component cost in half."

Also notice how the goals aren't the idea. At this stage, you don't think in terms of a solution, you simply want to clearly identify the need. There's a huge temptation to stop the process when a new idea pops into your head, but I strongly suggest you go ahead and complete your list of six goals.

What do you do with the six goals? Pick one (and only one) which you feel is most important to your prospect. Since you haven't even met yet, you must make a guess based on thorough research and thought, so go with your instincts. As you'll see when I work through the rest of the process, you can't really pick a *wrong* goal, so choose the one you feel strongest about. That single goal will be the basis for the idea you're going to propose. You'll use the other five for subsequent proposals, so don't throw away your notes!

Now, let's start coming up with ideas.

# CHAPTER 3

# UNLEASH
# YOUR IDEA POWER

et's talk about motivation. Why do customers buy from you? Is it because you're a smooth talker? Or because you have strong personal relationships with your clients? These attributes can't hurt, but you need more than just good looks and charm to sell a customer. You need ideas.

The main reason people buy from you is because you give them something of value. The most valuable item you can bring to clients is an idea to meet one of their needs or help them reach one of their goals. Ideas are motivators.

Now you're ready for the next step in the Creative Selling System. Step one is acquiring some basic knowledge about the client. Once you've learned about the basics of the client's business, you can develop a client goal to be reached or need to be satisfied. That's the second step. The third step is when you come up with an idea to reach that goal. I call this "ideation."

I'm careful to point out the three separate steps because one of the biggest temptations you face is coming up with an idea and immediately pitching it. But if the idea is not connected to a goal, you're going to be wrong a lot of the time. If you'll just do the first two steps—research the customer and come up with a goal—before you take the third step, you'll find that your ideas are a lot more accurate and much more attractive.

# DEMAND STAGE SELLING

Wouldn't it be great if you could read your customers' minds? You know, get inside their heads and walk around a little bit? The very best salespeople seem to have that ability—it's as if they know what customers are going to say before they say it. They have a sixth sense about which objections a particular customer is most likely to raise. They know what benefits ring the prospect's bell.

Some of this clairvoyant ability comes from experience, of course. Even more of it comes from advanced listening skills. Top salespeople really listen when their prospect is talking and pick up small cues that many people miss. Many good salespeople are also students of human psychology. They make it a point to study human nature and learn a lot about their customer in the process.

One important talent top salespeople have is the ability to recognize customers' demand stages and shape their presentations accordingly. They determine whether customers are getting ready to place an order or just starting to comparison shop. They can tell whether customers have already decided to buy the product and are negotiating for the best price or whether they're weighing other options. They understand that different things are important to the customer at each step in the buying process. They practice Demand Stage Selling.

Demand Stage Selling is a technique that identifies how far along in the buying process a customer has progressed. This tactic dictates that you create a presentation which appeals specifically to someone at each particular stage. Demand Stage Selling immediately helps block out irrelevant objections and tremendously improves your closing ratios.

## Three Stages Of Demand

Clients go through several stages in the decision process. First, they have to recognize a need and decide to buy something to fill that need. This decision creates primary demand. You can equate this stage to that little hunger pang you get in the late afternoon. Your need is the hunger, so you make a decision to purchase something to satisfy that hunger. You're experiencing primary demand.

Customers then have to decide on a type of product or service that will fill their need, thus creating secondary demand. *What* are

## MORE MONEY = MORE STAGES

**B**ig-ticket purchases often require a drawn out decision-making process that involves many smaller decisions within each demand stage. Consider automobiles. First, customers have to decide to buy a car. They may vacillate between the economy of repairing their old clunker and the ego boost of driving something new. While in this stage, car buyers get estimates for repairs, do some sticker shopping on car lots, and gather the opinions of friends and relatives.

They then have to decide what type of car they want. There are numerous choices to be made at this stage—new or used, sedan or SUV, front- or rear-wheel-drive, foreign or domestic, convertible or hard-top, etc. At this point, they collect brochures and magazine reviews, do a lot of test-driving, and generally frustrate the dealer's sales staff with their inability to give definite answers to questions about what they're looking for.

Finally, they have to choose a specific make and model and comparison shop before making the actual purchase. This may involve several visits and negotiating sessions. Buyers may compare dealers and investigate other ways to acquire a car, such as leasing or buying over the Internet.

As a rule, the larger the price tag, the more stages the buyer will go through to reach a final decision.

you hungry for? That's secondary demand—deciding how you're going to satisfy the primary demand. You have choices—a candy bar, a piece of fruit or some microwave popcorn.

Finally, the customer must decide which service provider or product brand to buy. This is third-level demand. In my afternoon snack example, this is when you decide whether to buy the Snickers or the Milky Way. You make the final purchase decision. In sales, this is the stage concentrated on most heavily.

## Match Sales Tactics To Demand Stages

There are many different kinds of selling, each of which influences different demand stages. There's transactional selling, which focuses on filling orders efficiently. There's negotiation, which concentrates on securing the greatest share of business at the most profitable price points. Both of these occur at the third level of demand. There's also missionary selling, which aims to create new primary or secondary demand through educating customers.

Sometimes you make presentations that attempt to persuade prospective clients to choose your need-satisfying mechanism. For example, the TV network salesperson presents reasons prospects should use TV advertising instead of radio, without crowing about the network's ratings. This is a clear attempt to create secondary demand. Prospects have already made the decision to advertise (having self-identified a need), and the salesperson is trying to influence their decision on which medium to use. The grand strategy, of course, is that the salesperson will get a fair share of the buy if his or her medium is chosen.

> The most common mistake is to apply a universal sales approach to all prospects.

It's easy to confuse the different types of selling and expect the tools and techniques that apply to one to apply to another. It's also easy to incorrectly identify a customer's demand stage and take the wrong approach.

Most of the time, you concentrate so hard on getting market share and securing the easy order, you forget to create new business—or you try to create primary or secondary demand using tools aimed at the third demand stage (e.g., pricing). Sometimes you concentrate so much on getting new customers that you forget to upsell your current customers. This can lead to growth-killing customer turnover. The most common mistake is to apply a universal sales approach to all prospects regardless of their demand stage.

## Idea Selling *Always* Applies

There is only one way to influence all three stages of the demand creation process: Sell ideas! When you sell ideas, you create primary demand by identifying the client's needs—it's part of the idea development process. You also create secondary demand by presenting an idea related to your type of need-satisfaction. You most certainly create third-level demand by selling ideas that your competitors can't offer.

One of the biggest obstacles faced by most salespeople and marketing organizations is persuading more clients to enter the market. That's why it's so hard to make cold calls. Prospects who need a missionary-type pitch, but get a third-level demand presentation, aren't likely to bite because they don't perceive a need for the product. Think of it this way: If you don't need a car (say you recently bought one), would you buy another one just because the salesman made a good pitch? Of course not.

Most salespeople aren't usually trying to create primary demand when they cold call. They're really making as many calls as possible in hopes of stumbling across a few prospects who have already made the primary demand-creating decision to buy something, but just haven't decided what to buy. Typical cold-callers then hard-sell the prospect that's already in the market, securing the sale instead of allowing a competitor to get it. In the meantime, the salesperson wastes a great deal of time and effort making the wrong type of pitch to other prospects.

Why do so many salespeople work this way? It's because persuading the prospect that they have a need is the most difficult hurdle to overcome. If I'm not hungry, it does no good to pitch me on a candy bar. But if you waved a little chocolate under my nose, it might stimulate my hunger. It's the same way with ideas. When you can show the prospect an idea, or a new way of looking at the possibilities for their business, they might recognize a need they didn't see before.

# FINDING IDEAS

Creative sellers with open minds have an endless market for their ideas. But most people don't consider themselves creative enough to come up with good ideas. Their minds stop working when someone asks for an idea.

Some people actually have lots of ideas but are hesitant to use them because they're afraid they won't be good enough. They don't offer their ideas, so they never get any positive feedback, and since they don't get any feedback, they don't offer their ideas. The loop is closed.

The problem with that kind of thinking is that it puts the onus of judgment on the wrong person. The salesperson shouldn't judge the merits of an idea—leave that to the prospect. If the customer thinks it's good—it's good! Put the idea in front of them using the best presentation skills you have and let the prospect make the final judgment.

Stop worrying about being wrong and start taking a few chances. If one prospect doesn't like the idea, take the same idea to the next one. "Bad ideas" are just ideas that haven't been sold yet, so keep pitching them. Like any good matchmaker, you'll eventually put the right prospect with the right idea.

## Brainstorming

To come up with ideas to sell, you need to continually practice brainstorming. You've probably been in brainstorming meetings with your management and other salespeople. The techniques I'm talking about are the same ones you use in a group meeting, only I explore their use on an individual level. It's great to participate in group sessions, but you can't rely on them to generate all your ideas.

Here are the steps: Start by writing down your prospect's goal. On the page below it, make a list of possible ways your company's products or services could help the prospect reach that goal. Follow

### BRAINSTORMING 101

You don't need a group of people to brainstorm. You can do it by yourself if you just open your mind and let it create. Just heed the four golden rules of brainstorming:

1. **There's no such thing as a bad idea.** Write it down even if it's impossible. Especially write it down if anyone in the room says, "We've never done that before." Reserve judgment until later.

2. **See how outrageous you can be.** Associate freely and write it down. The wilder the idea, the better. Crazy ideas spark more ideas—mundane ones are dead ends.

3. **Fill the page—then start another one.** Quantity is your goal because the more ideas you list, the better the odds of finding a good one.

4. **Don't stop when you come to the "right" idea.** There could well be a better one waiting to come out.

the ground rules of successful brainstorming while you're writing, (see "Brainstorming 101" on page 34).

In the next step, review the ideas and combine or extend them, creating new ideas through the interplay of the elements of other ideas. Again, don't be judgmental. It's not time to throw out bad ideas. This combining and extending process should add ideas to your list of possibilities, not remove them.

There are several ways to stimulate your brainstorm production. Look inside the company for internal solutions. Many companies package their products or create bundles of services that are designed to meet the needs of certain categories of customers. You certainly don't want to ignore those. The only caution is to be sure the pre-packaged offering fits your prospect's particular goal. You may need to tweak the package to make it work.

Another source is free association with nonrelated concepts. This is a fancy term for stealing an idea from someplace else. One of my associates monitors TV commercials and thumbs through magazine ads to see if there's a slogan or concept he can use to springboard his own idea. For example, he'll take a character like Tony the Tiger and create an animated cat named Karla the Kitten who purrs "You'rrre grrrand" when its owner feeds it Brand X. Or he'll take a slogan like "You're in good hands with Allstate" and come up with "You're in good form with Diet Rite." He's not exactly stealing the other person's idea, just using it to spark his own.

Another way to start this process is by examining past sales to like customers. Don't look at the dollars and cents or the unit volume. Look deeper and see if you can determine or surmise why the customer made that purchase. Talk to the salespeople. Pick their brains about the circumstances and events that led to the sale. Sales veterans are usually full of stories about their battles and victories. Next time you're subjected to a war story, see if you can detect an idea that sparked the battle.

## Choose An Idea

The third step is to choose the one idea you feel most confident presenting. It should open a clear and direct path to the prospect's goal. Judge the idea by its ability to achieve the desired goal. Don't worry about nonrelevant standards, like whether it's ever been done before. All you need to be concerned about is the idea's ability to

## No Garden Variety Idea

Y ou've selected your goal for your first proposal. Now, let's brainstorm some ideas. Here's a list of six possible marketing ideas you can sell a retail garden shop that raise the quality of the shop's merchandise in the mind of its best customer:

1. Run an ad campaign stressing the name brands the store carries. National brands often denote quality to the consumer.

2. Adopt and publicize a new slogan for the store: "We Sell the Best for Less" on all ads, signage, stationery, etc.

3. Build an ad campaign around customer testimonials about the quality of plants purchased from your prospect's store.

4. Sponsor a "bountiful garden" contest where customers submit the largest vegetables they raised from seed or seedlings purchased from the prospect.

5. Place ads spoofing the Good Housekeeping Seal of Approval for quality, awarding the prospect's store the Good Gardener's Seal of Approval.

6. Create an animated flower character, Rose Trueheart, for a spokesperson in a series of TV commercials.

See how easy that is? This is a list of six different ideas, any one of which accomplish your goal. Rose Trueheart may not be the next Ronald McDonald, but she may be the final piece to your marketing puzzle.

accomplish the prospect's goal, your company's ability to execute the idea, and the idea's profitability to the prospect and your company.

There is one final check to make before preparing your presentation. See if you can clearly express your idea in a sentence or two. Try to say it aloud without taking a breath. If you can't, re-examine the idea to see if it's too complicated. It may be too confusing for the prospect. Remember, you're preparing for a first-call presentation. Your goal is to make a strong and favorable first impression. Overwhelming a prospect with a proposal that you can't explain in simple terms is a sure way to lose a follow-up call.

Can you use this ideation process if you sell widgets or fixtures or insurance? Why not? Don't your prospective customers have related needs: growing sales, cutting costs, raising employee morale? Of course they do. If not, your product or service wouldn't exist. Open your mind to the possibilities.

You've come up with the ideas, now pick one and pitch it. That's right. Pick one—any one. It doesn't matter which idea you choose as long as you know your company can deliver it. You can't choose one based on your knowledge of the customer's likes and dislikes because you haven't met the prospect—so just pick one and pitch it.

## The Secret Of The First Call

That's when you'll learn the real secret to creative selling. Your real goal on the first call is not necessarily to sell that first idea—it's to gather accurate information about the prospect. That way, your subsequent ideas will hit the mark.

As you gather information, you're also accomplishing several other things. You will make a strong first impression by demonstrating a willingness to invest *your* time in a study of *their* needs. You will establish yourself as an idea resource. If you bring prospects something of value in return for their time, they are likely to see you again. Above all, your idea will provoke a discussion about the prospect's needs, desires, goals and opportunities. It's through that discussion that you learn what they will buy from you.

## Stockpile Ideas

Remember all those ideas you didn't use? Just like the unused goals from the needs analysis step, save them for later. The presentation you're preparing is just the first of many you'll be making to this prospect. The prospect may not buy your idea on the first call, so you'll need another one. Even if the sale does happen, you may want to have those ideas available for further development of the account through add-on sales or contract extensions. Either way, you always need more ideas.

Another reason to keep all the unused goals and ideas on file is their value to you in working on other prospects. The creative selling process is very effort-intense. You'll invest a couple hours of research and ideation into each proposal. It's much more profitable to amortize that investment over several prospects rather than just one. You probably have other potential customers who are in similar, if not identical, businesses. You'll find their needs similar. Getting the most results from the amount of work expended is a principle of good time management.

> If you're selling the same solvent to the same customer at the same time year after year, it's hard to get very excited.

Many sales departments have a central file of ideas used by all their salespeople. The background research and needs analysis are also available in the file. Every time an idea-based proposal is created, it goes into this file and the entire team can then draw on it (if it isn't bought by the first prospect). From the company's standpoint, such a system creates a valuable asset for future growth. From the salesperson's perspective, it prevents duplicating efforts already made by others.

As you can imagine, there are plenty of methods for organizing and accessing this valuable resource. They can range from index cards to databases. Even salespeople who work in relatively isolated territories can pool their ideas through the Internet. No matter what form it takes, the keys to building this resource are volume and team work. Everyone has to pitch in. If not, the major contributors will feel unfairly treated and keep their research and ideas to themselves.

## Your Motivation

Ideation has another benefit besides creating good customer relations. It keeps your job interesting. There's an old sales adage that says when you first start out, you're 90 percent enthusiasm and 10 percent knowledge. After you have sold for awhile, it changes to 90 percent knowledge and 10 percent enthusiasm. The trade-off for gaining the knowledge is losing the enthusiasm.

If you're selling the same solvent to the same customer at the same time year after year, it's hard to get very excited about the next sale. Can you imagine the customer's excitement level? But if you're constantly challenging yourself to come up with a new use for that solvent or a safer way to dispose of it, your enthusiasm for both the product and the customer will go up. In turn, so will the customer's.

Get out before the next truck comes along and grinds you deeper into a rut. Become an idea seller. Learn the skills of ideation and practice them. You'll never grow bored with your job because you'll be putting something new into it every day.

# CHAPTER 4

# YOU AND MARK TWAIN

**N**ow it's time to put your idea on paper. You ultimately make the sale through an oral presentation, but expressing your idea in writing has its advantages. Writing a proposal is kind of like broccoli—you may not like it, but you know it's good for you.

Preparing a written presentation helps clarify the details of your concept. Many times the writing will reveal a hidden weakness in your idea that can be corrected before you pitch it. It may change your thinking about which are the strongest points and lead you to reorder or restructure the pitch to highlight them. In either case, a written proposal is a form of rehearsal that makes you more familiar and comfortable with the idea you are selling. It increases your confidence in the idea, resulting in a more forceful oral presentation.

The fact that you prepared a written presentation can also encourage the prospect to buy. One of my clients in Nebraska reported that one of his prospects knew which proposals to take seriously because they always had a cover page. Writing takes time and effort. Most people hate to write almost as much as they dread speaking in front of groups. Your prospects are no different. They'll recognize your investment in their proposal more readily when they see the written work you've put into it.

The written presentation demonstrates to the prospect that you're willing to spend a great deal of your time and energy on their behalf. Your professionalism and dedication to getting the details right will impress them as long as it looks (and sounds) good.

The written presentation serves as the prospect's tangible reminder of your oral presentation. Very few of your prospects are going to give you an answer on your first call. They're going to want to think about it. While they're "thinking," you want them to be able to refer to a persuasive outline of your proposal. That proposal needs to highlight the same things you stress in your oral presentation—the benefits of your idea.

During your oral pitch, the written presentation focuses the prospect's thinking on the points you want them to see, in the order you want them considered. The presentation keeps them from jumping to the price before they've seen the benefits. It provides a visual link between the idea and its benefits. Above all, it reinforces and lends greater credibility to the points you make orally. Many people still believe a written statement is more trustworthy than an oral one.

Finally, the written presentation serves as a script for you to follow during your oral presentation. Having it with you while you're talking gives you greater confidence and helps you stay on track. It frees you from having to remember what comes next. The written presentation helps you cover *all* the points you want to make. In sales, there are few worse feelings than remembering a key point you wanted to make, while walking back to your car.

Those are the advantages of developing a strong written presentation. So how do you go about it?

# BEGINNING YOUR PRESENTATION

At the risk of sounding like your ninth grade English teacher, let's start by developing an outline. List the points you want to make and develop a format to meet the goal of your presentation. You want to convince the prospect that a need exists and that your proposal satisfies it. The work you did assessing needs and creating ideas are the beginning elements of the outline. You can use the form on page 45 to help you.

At the top of the page, put your prospect's name in nice, big letters. You should keep that in front of you at all times. This ensures that you remain focused on the customer. You're also going to use

## WHAT'S IN IT FOR ME?

It's important to keep in mind that benefits are different from features. Customers buy products not to acquire the product itself but to get the benefits that product provides. In other words, customers buy electric drills to make holes, not to simply add another power tool to their collection. You know whether an item is a feature or a benefit if it answers the question, "What's it going to do for me?"

| Feature | Benefit |
|---------|---------|
| High horsepower motor | Drills faster with fewer binds |
| Large capacity chuck | Accepts larger bits to drill larger holes |
| Long battery life | Cuts interruptions for battery change |
| Ergonomic design | Reduces fatigue and soreness |

Truly creative salespeople not only know every feature of their products but also what the customer gets from those features.

Read the benefits list you just made. Are there any features on it? If so, turn them into benefits by answering the question, "What's this feature do for the customer?" You want to list the results not the causes.

this one-page outline for your written presentation, so you'll want this reminder in a few minutes.

The next item on the outline is your goal. Once again, write it down in a sentence or two.

Next comes the idea you came up with to help the prospect achieve the goal. You've already done this step, so you're really just copying the work you did in the previous chapter.

Now list the benefits of the idea. What's in it for the prospect who buys your idea? You'll want to list at least three benefits (but no more than four). These are bullet points, so they must be concise and self-explanatory. Here's a big hint: The first benefit accomplishes the prime goal you just wrote down. The rest are related but of lesser importance.

Now list the elements you need the prospect to buy in order to get these benefits. This is where you outline the package of products or services you're going to sell, along with any "behind the sale" actions that you or your company need to take to execute the idea.

Think of this not just as a product description but as a checklist for delivering the product. For example, if you're selling a marketing promotion that includes a contest, you'll need entry forms, prizes and rules, as well as media to promote it, which entails ad production and media buying. If you're selling a piece of manufacturing software, you may need to provide an interface with the customer's computer system, in addition to training, manuals, installation or other related items. Once again, these are just your notes, so make these bullet points rather than paragraphs. Just make sure to list *everything* you may need.

## Setting Your Price

It's time for the final element of the outline: the dollar value. You'll use the checklist you made above to price the package. You'll use whatever pricing latitude you have and follow whatever guidelines you use for negotiation, volume discounts or special offers.

Now, here's where that estimate of customer potential comes in. How does the price for your execution of the idea—including all the elements you just listed—compare with the customer potential estimate? If it exceeds it, you may have a problem. You'll need to rethink your idea to take it out of the realm of wishful thinking and put it back into the category of the possible. Remember, one of the main reasons for doing the estimate is to make sure you're presenting something the customer can afford.

> Build a proposal that's worth at least half the dollars you came up with in the estimate.

But what if the price of the idea is only a small percentage of its estimated potential? Same drill: Rework or rethink the idea to bring it into line with the prospect. My rule of thumb is to go for no less than 50 percent of the prospect's potential annual spending on your product or service. In other words, build a proposal that's worth at least half the dollars you came up with in the estimate.

You may want to propose a deal that's more or less than a year in length, depending on the purchase cycle in your industry. Use the 50 percent goal as your base and adjust your proposal accordingly.

# PROPOSAL OUTLINE FORM

1. Prospect Name

_____

2. Prospect Goal

_____

_____

_____

_____

3. Idea

_____

_____

_____

_____

4. Benefits of the Idea

_____

_____

_____

_____

5. Execution Elements

_____

_____

_____

_____

_____

6. Proposal Price

_____

_____

Many salespeople are inclined to back away from such an aggressive tactic, especially with new prospects. They'll argue that they need a small proposal to get their foot in the door—to give prospects a taste of what they can really do or to let them get used to doing business with the salespeople. These are rationalizations of the worst sort. They make no logical business sense. What these salespeople are really saying is that they don't have much faith in their product. They want to sell the prospect a sample because then the prospect won't be as unhappy if the product doesn't meet expectations.

Creative salespeople have the courage of their convictions. If your widget is the answer to the prospect's most pressing need, why wait for them to try a sample? Is delayed gratification a virtue? What kind of favor are you doing the customer?

If you don't believe in your product, you will never have a successful sales career. Not that you won't make a living—you may even make a good one. It's just that you won't get much job satisfaction. If you lack faith in what you sell, you are labeling yourself a liar every time you try to sell it and a fraud every time you complete a sale. If you don't believe your product does what you claim, do yourself, your customers and your company a favor: Find another line of work.

## LESS IS NEVER MORE

Have you ever tried to raise money for a new opportunity? Banks, venture capitalists—even deep-pocketed private investors won't consider requests for less than tens of millions of dollars, no matter how secure and profitable the loan or investment is. In addition, they can only properly investigate so many deals each year. It takes just as long to look over a $100,000 application as it does a $100 million application.

The same is true for your proposals. If you want to get your prospect's attention, ask for a million dollars. That's the kind of decision the top person makes. If you want to spend the rest of your life selling to the second assistant night co-manager at the West Fork branch, try to pitch the top decision maker a $1000 proposal. You'll be delegated to West Fork immediately.

Many salespeople who undersell their product or service just don't believe that their customers could possibly have the potential they've estimated. This self-defeating attitude can be attributed to a general lack of knowledge. It's shocking how many salespeople—even experienced ones—don't give their customers and prospects credit for running large, successful businesses.

It's human nature to view prospects through the filter of your own experience. As successful salespeople, you make a good living—maybe well into six figures. You know how hard you have to work and how much effort goes into producing that sum. You also know how much dollar volume you have to produce to create that salary. You may find it hard to imagine someone else making multiples of your income, except in a theoretical sense. Unless you ran a business like your prospect's or gained firsthand knowledge of their financial statements, it's difficult to picture their reality.

Misperceptions lead some salespeople to internalize the buying decision. They try to put themselves in the customer's shoes and judge the proposal through the customer's eyes. This is normally a very good step to take, but it can lead to problems if you're not objective. Unfortunately, it's easy to let your judgment be determined by the size of your own pocketbook, rather than the potential of the prospect's. With many products or services, you may propose a sum in excess of your annual income. It's easy to confuse your vision with your customer's.

> Small proposals get delegated to the lackeys and flak-catchers.

Whatever the reason, making a proposal too small is a very common obstacle to sales success. Big-dollar proposals send the message that they are important. That means the important decision makers need to see them. Small proposals have the opposite effect—they get delegated to the lackeys and flak-catchers.

Big proposals have the potential of making major impacts on the prospect's business, so they get a much higher level of consideration than small ones, which are often seen as more trouble than they are worth. This is especially true when you're selling to major corporations.

Think about what's necessary to move the needle on the sales of a small company—one with $200 million in annual sales. A "measly" 5 percent gain is $10 million. If you're selling a product or service that's supposed to increase your prospect's sales, you better show

how it contributes to a significant part of that growth. If not, your proposal won't get serious consideration.

Maybe your product's main benefit is improved profitability. If that $200 million prospect has a 40 percent gross profit margin, the scale you're working on is $80 million. How far will your idea move *that* needle? Look at the numbers for your prospect's estimated annual revenues and ask yourself what impact your idea could have on them. That will tell you the importance of your idea to the prospect and how it ranks among others he might consider.

This concept is crucial to the success of the salesperson using the Creative Selling System. If you're inclined to undersell, overcome this problem by addressing it head-on. Prepare estimates of prospects' potential and adjust your proposals accordingly.

# THE STANDARD 5-PAGE PROPOSAL

It's time to turn your outline into the finished product: the pieces of paper you show the client. This should be easy, because you've already done most of the hard work. The standard proposal in the Creative Selling System has five pages. There may be other printed material used to supplement it, but the heart of the proposal is just five pages.

## Page 1

The first page is the cover page. It contains what you might expect: the prospect's name, your company's name, and contact information such as your address, phone/fax number and e-mail address. If your company provides cover pages for proposals (complete with logos and pictures), make sure the largest item on the page is the prospect's name—larger than your company's logo and larger than the picture of your product. That's why you write the prospect's name at the top of your outline—to remind you that the customer is the focus.

## Page 2

The second page contains the benefits of the proposal. Copy the benefits you wrote on the outline and list them as prominent bullet points. You might have a headline with the prospect's name, but that's the only other item. This page won't have much on it, but it's such a key part of the Creative Selling System that you will use it twice.

## Page 3

The third page is the idea page. Here's where you explain what you're going to do for the prospect and how you're going to do it. The goal of the idea page is to convince the prospect that your idea will deliver the benefits you've promised on the preceding page. This page is free-form, since every product or service has different ways of presenting itself. You may want to use paragraphs and full sentences, bullet points or a combination. Just make sure you cover all the elements of execution listed on your outline.

Here's where you present your selling points in persuasive language. Weave the prospect's name into the text as often as possible, and make the explanation as clear as you can. The idea page carries the reasons your ideas work. It also gives arguments for buying your product or service.

The idea page needs to be clear and simple to read. A good rule of thumb is that a first-time buyer of your product should be able to understand your idea simply by reading this page. In fact, one of the best tests of whether you have accomplished this is to find someone—your spouse, a friend, or anyone who is not familiar with the intricacies of your product—to read this page and tell you what it says.

Here's an absolute rule: The idea page can be no more than one page long. If you can't explain what your idea does for the prospect in one page, your idea is too complicated. Complex proposals with lots of minor decisions and multiple options take a long time to get approved. In my book, K.I.S.S. also stands for Keep It Sellable, Stupid.

## Page 4

The fourth page is the proposal page, which answers the dollars and cents questions. Nothing up to this point included a price tag. Now you're going to lay it out in such a way that it lends credibility to your presentation. Don't look at price as an obstacle, but rather as an aid.

## FIVE QUICK PAGES

Here's a checklist of the five pages in your creative selling proposal:

❑ Page 1: Cover with prospect name

❑ Page 2: Benefits of your idea

❑ Page 3: How your idea works

❑ Page 4: How much does your idea costs

❑ Page 5: Benefits of your idea

The first part of the page should specify the length of time covered by the agreement, list what you're including in the package, and provide all the contractual information such as delivery dates, quantities, qualities and grades. This page should also detail who is responsible for what actions—who's going to install the software or purchase the contest prizes, for example. It contains all the information the prospect needs to make a decision.

The one thing this page doesn't contain is unit pricing. Prospects need to know the total cost of the idea, of course, but they don't need to know how much each element costs. You have already presented them with a complete package to solve their problems. Each element is integral, but the idea is offered as a whole, not piecemeal.

The only reason they need unit prices is so they can negotiate the individual items to arrive at a lower price or to pick and choose the ones they want. They may even substitute a competitor's item for one of yours. If prospects insist on having that data, you're going to give it to them, but only after you've completed this presentation and secured an agreement from them that the idea is something they want. Don't put unit prices in the proposal.

This tactic is also a way to keep the prospect focused on the merits of the idea. If they start examining the minutiae of unit pricing, they easily lose sight of the big picture—your idea. Only put items you want to discuss on the agenda.

What about the total price? That will be readily available, of course. I suggest that it be expressed in some other terms than the "Grand Total." Even billionaires are subject to sticker shock, so I like to present the price in increments. "Investment per month" or "budget per location" is usually an easier pill to swallow. That's the figure that's printed on your proposal, never the "Grand Total." When the prospect reaches for a calculator to multiply the budget by the number of locations, you step in and tell them the total. Don't put it on the page. The total should be on your lips, not on your paper.

This serves another purpose. If you've ever watched prospects' eyes when handed a proposal, you know they immediately go to the bottom of each page. They instinctively look for the price and keep that figure in the front of their minds. Everything you say is filtered through the context of the price. In fact, they may spend the entire pitch preparing to slam you with a price objection, ignoring the many brilliant points you're making. By leaving this grand total off the page, you're denying the prospect this opportunity.

# Page 5

The fifth and final page of the written proposal is the easiest of all—it's just a copy of the benefits page. Make two copies and use one of them as the last page. This final page is the one you want prospects to look at when you ask them for the order. The page you don't want them fixed on is the proposal page, which has the price. At the end, put the benefits page in front of them again.

You want the prospect to say yes or no to the benefits you're offering, not to spending money. It's a subtle point, but one that's at the heart of all good selling. You use the written proposal as both your script and as your major visual aid during your oral presentation. It's best to ask for the order while the prospect is reviewing the benefits.

## SAMPLE PROPOSAL

On the following pages is a sample proposal in my five-page format. This proposal is designed to sell an advertising program to a hospital. You'll notice it's pretty simple. The proposal entails a year-long TV advertising campaign, extensive video production, awards and giveaways, and many other details. The idea is explained completely in one page and the proposal of $120,000 is outlined in another.

# Creatively Marketing

# St. Luke's Hospital

# A Marketing Plan from
# WSDA-TV

**For further information, contact:**
Dave Donelson
(999) 999-9999
fax (999) 999-9999

*Sample Cover Page*

Here's an idea for St. Luke's Hospital that will...

○ Maintain and enhance the caring reputation the hospital has earned throughout your service area.

○ Increase inpatient occupancy.

○ Promote the usage of outpatient services.

○ Encourage and further raise the morale of the volunteers who serve the patients in St. Luke's Hospital.

*Sample Benefits Page*

The concept is simple. Each month, St. Luke's Hospital will select a volunteer group for special recognition on WSDA-TV.

WSDA-TV will air a 90-second video salute to the group, followed by a 30-second commercial that promotes one of St. Luke's units or services.

These messages will air as a two-minute block isolated from other commercials. This ensures greater viewer attention and involvement.

Following is a suggested schedule of Volunteer Groups and Units:

| Month | Group | Unit |
|-------|-------|------|
| Jan. | Methodist Church | Pediatric |
| Feb. | Candy stripers | Cardiac |
| Mar. | Kiwanis | Long-Term |
| Apr. | St. Luke's Auxiliary | OB/GYN |
| May | Sweet Adeline's | Geriatrics |
| June | Rotary | Health Club |
| July | Baptist Church | Ontology |
| Aug. | Community Theater | Emergency |
| Sep. | Optimists | Outpatient Rehab |
| Oct. | Lion's Club | Sports Medicine |
| Nov. | Knights of Columbus | Hospice |
| Dec. | Unitarian Church | Burn Care |

At the end of the year, WSDA-TV will sponsor a banquet with St. Luke's to honor all volunteer groups at the hospital. A highlight of the banquet will be a showing of the 12 vignettes produced during the year. We will also provide each group with a copy of that video for their own use.

This program puts the powerful impact of television behind St. Luke's message. It uses all of TV's communications tools—sight, sound, motion, and the full range of human emotion—to spread the word that St. Luke's is the most sympathetic caregiver in the market. This year-long program not only promotes St. Luke's services but conveys to the community that the hospital is the home of many caring, giving staff and volunteers.

*Sample Idea Page*

# St. Luke's Hospital

Proposed Annual WSDA TV Schedule

| Day/Time | Program | #/Week |
|---|---|---|
| M-F 7:00-9:00 a.m. | Network This Morning | 2 |
| M-F 3:00-4:00 p.m. | Talk Show of the Day | 1 |
| M-F 4:00-5:00 p.m. | Famous People Talk Show | 1 |
| M-F 5:00-5:30 p.m. | First Edition News | 2 |
| M-F 6:00-6:30 p.m. | WSDA Early News | 1 |
| M-F 6:30-7:00 p.m. | Young Adult Sitcom | 1 |
| M-S 10:00-10:30 p.m. | WSDA Late News | 1 |
| M-F 10:30-11:00 p.m. | Older Appeal Sitcom | 1 |

**Your investment includes:**

○ Total Messages:   520 / Year

○ Video Production:  12 Volunteer Vignette

12 Unit Commercials

○ Volunteer Banquet for 100

*Monthly Investment:*   $9,965

This program begins January 1 and runs through December 31, 200X.

*Sample Dollar Proposal Page*

Here's an idea for St. Luke's Hospital that will...

○ Maintain and enhance the caring reputation the hospital has earned throughout your service area.

○ Increase inpatient occupancy.

○ Promote the usage of outpatient services.

○ Encourage and further raise the morale of the volunteers who serve the patients in St. Luke's Hospital.

*Sample Last Benefits Page*

## Support Material

The format of the written proposal contains answers to two questions directly pertaining to the prospect's buying decision: 1) What's it going to do for me? and 2) How much does it cost? Anything else is superfluous. In fact, cluttering up proposals with company histories, mission statements, and maps of your worldwide plant locations distracts prospects from the job at hand: buying your idea. All these things have their place in the selling process, but that place isn't on the prospect's desk while you're asking for the order.

The only other material you might want to have in addition to the basic five-page written proposal is a demonstration. You can add something like a sample of the reports generated by your software or a storyboard of your TV commercial. Make sure your presentation is produced just for this prospect—that way, it enhances rather than detracts from your status as an expert working for the prospect's benefit. You won't be seen as a peddler trying to move unsold inventory.

These support materials should not be part of the written proposal. Keep them on hand, and use them separately to keep from distracting the prospect.

## The Final Step

There's one last step in preparing your written presentation: Proofread it—then have someone else proofread it. These few pages make a powerful impression. Maintain a zero-tolerance policy when it comes to misspellings and grammatical errors. Nothing creates a negative impression faster than a sloppy proposal.

Proofreading isn't just reading over the material. You have to isolate each word and sentence and check it against your mental dictionary (then against a real one if there's the slightest doubt). Don't rely on your computer's grammar or spell-checker—they're notorious for missing simple mistakes. "You scan have this find produce reel cheep" has five typos that make the writer sound like an idiot—but it will pass both the grammar and spell-checking programs of most word processing software.

To put a spin on an old carpenter's adage: Write once, proofread twice.

# ALTERNATIVE PROPOSALS

An old sales theory says you should offer prospects three proposals: one for more than you think they want to spend, one for much less, and one for what you really expect them to buy.

The reasoning behind this theory is that the prospect won't buy the little proposal because it makes them look cheap. They won't buy the biggest one because they can't, but they will buy the middle one because it's the safest choice. Compared to the biggest one, it looks like a bargain.

This approach may be fine for some types of products or services, but I believe it seriously undermines your credibility. When you practice creative selling, you present yourself as an expert in your field. You send the message that you have studied your prospects' situations, analyzed their opportunities and problems, and used your expertise to come up with the optimum plan for each of them.

How can there be three best plans? When you give the prospect three different proposals, aren't you saying that you're not confident in your ability to make a strong recommendation?

A similar tactic is to give the prospect Proposal A while keeping Proposal B in your briefcase. Proposal B is always smaller, of course, and it's the one you whip out at the first sign of a price objection. This tactic sends two really bad signals. The first one we've already covered: What kind of an expert can't give you the best alternative?

The second signal you're sending is the real killer. Having seen Proposal A and Proposal B, prospects will think Proposal C is waiting in the wings, and will appear only if they give the salesperson enough resistance. Way to go—you've just created your own price objection.

There's another big danger in using either of these methods. Faced with choices, most of us delay making a decision. In fact, some people hate making decisions so much, they actually welcome more choices, just to delay making a final decision.

Any salesperson knows that the most frustrating customer isn't the one who says no, it's the one who says maybe. Why give the customer an excuse to "think it over?" Give them *one* proposal so they can give you *one* answer. It'll simplify your life, and you'll be shocked at what it does for your time management skills.

# CHAPTER 5

# ENTER THE INNER SANCTUM

re you ready to sell? Have you have researched your prospect's business? Have you estimated the potential spending, identified a probable need for your product, and developed an idea? Have you polished and proofread your written presentation? If you can answer yes to all these questions, you're ready to enter the Inner Sanctum.

Here's where most new salespeople (and plenty of experienced ones, too), make a mistake. They're eager to get the process started and they've got a lot of things to do, so they rush out and drop in on the prospect, saying something like "I was in your neighborhood, so I thought I'd stop by and see if you wanted to hear about this great idea I have for you." This is not a great way to make a good first impression.

Others take the time to make an appointment but blow it by calling ahead with a pitch like "Hello, I'd like to show you our newest line of widgets. When can you see me?" They wonder why The Boss is always too busy to see them—and why they always seem to get his voice mail when they call back.

At least the second salesperson demonstrated some professionalism by making an appointment. The first one apparently didn't place enough value on the prospect's time to reserve some of it in advance.

When you drop in on a prospect, you and your proposal are placed in the same category as all the other salespeople who work without appointments—little girls peddling cookies, political pamphleteers, and the door-to-door vacuum salesperson. All these people serve important functions in the overall scheme of our economy, but do you really want your $120,000 idea considered along with the latest line of peanut butter fudge cookies?

# MAKING COLD-CALL APPOINTMENTS

If you want to build a reputation as a top-notch professional, you must treat your clientele accordingly. Respect the value of their time and put a value on yours: Make an appointment! It sends all the right messages: You're important, I'm important, and my idea is important enough to set aside some of your day to consider it.

## Getting Past The Screener

The most difficult part of making an appointment is just getting an opportunity to talk to your prospect. Few prospects answer their own phone or take calls from people they don't know. I've found that contact is made with the prospect in only 16 percent of initial call attempts. The rest of the time, I had to leave a message. You can count on failing to make contact in at least four out of every five calls.

---

### RECIPE FOR EASY COLD-CALLS

There are five ingredients you should use in all of your appointment telephone calls. Using them consistently will increase your effectiveness and set the perfect tone for your meeting with the prospect.

1. Get permission.

2. Share your enthusiasm.

3. Promise a reward.

4. Guarantee no obligation.

5. Close your appointment.

---

Despite the odds, you still need to make an appointment. So you call and ask to speak to The Boss. The person on the other end of the phone—if you're lucky enough to get a person—says "No, you can't talk to The Boss now." That person is the screener. Screeners say the same thing to everybody because that's their job. What do you do?

First, make sure you're not sabotaging your call. It sounds crazy, but I've heard salespeople say things like "Is The Boss available, or is she busy?" or even "May I speak with The Boss, or is she doing something important right now?"

Openings like these reduce the screener's perception of your importance and value. You need to take the opposite approach. Make it sound like a telephone conversation with you is the most important thing The Boss can do.

Be assertive. Let the screener know how valuable your call is. In the Creative Selling System, you're always selling ideas, so offer one as a reward to The Boss for returning your call. Say something like:

"Hi, this is Dave Donelson with SDA, and I've got a great advertising idea to give to The Boss. May I speak with her, please?"

Now, you're a giver of value, not just a consumer of time. State your request with confidence. Assume the close. Expect to be connected right away. Don't be cocky, just confident. After you make your offer, let the screener respond.

Getting through screeners is a lot like making the sale—you need some information before you can close the deal. Encourage them to talk. See how much information you can get. If the screener asks you to leave a message, ask a few polite questions:

❍ Oh, is she in today?

❍ Is she out of the building?

❍ What time do you expect the meeting to be over?

❍ Do you expect her to go to her desk after the meeting?

These queries will help you reach the decision maker. As long as you're polite and conversational, most people will give you useful information.

Asking questions works because screeners don't expect it. Since they are giving you a standard brush-off, they expect one in response. If you don't just give them your name and number (which is what they expect), you open the door to informative communication.

The best response to the brush-off is persistence. You have to show screeners that you aren't going away. To get rid of you, they have to answer some questions.

You're still going to have to leave a message with the screener, so be polite. Watch your tone. Remember to stress that you want to give something to The Boss, not just take up her time.

It's perfectly natural to be reluctant about cold-calls, but there is a well-practiced formula that will help you overcome your reluctance and get the appointment once you're past the screener. There are five rules to the process.

# Rule 1: Get Permission

One of the biggest fears about cold calling is getting lumped with those pesky salespeople who call at dinner time with the latest long distance calling plan. What kind of reception do you give those people? How well do you listen? How much consideration do you give to what they are saying?

These callers are intruders into your life—they don't have your permission. To avoid being put in that category, find a good time to talk to the prospect. It's a courtesy that affords you the respect and attention you deserve.

To get permission, ask if the prospect has a minute to speak with you—not to buy anything—just to make an appointment for a short meeting in person. Find a phrase you like, then use it on all your calls. "Is this a good time to talk?" or "May I have about a minute?" are good starters. My personal favorite is "I know you're busy, so I'll only take a minute."

# Rule 2: Share Your Enthusiasm

Your next step is to share your enthusiasm. We commonly think of communication as an exchange of information between two or more people. But truly *persuasive* communication—as in sales—requires sharing enthusiasm, not just information. It's never more true than when you're on the telephone.

Prospects have to know you're excited about this particular call. They don't want to feel like just the next number on a long list. What you say is important, but the excitement you convey is more important when it comes to getting an appointment.

## THE DISC JOCKEY'S SECRET

There are a couple of simple tricks I learned when I worked as a radio announcer that help in all telephone work. First, stand up and move around when you're talking on the phone. Standing increases your circulation and energy. You also breathe more deeply, which puts more power in your voice.

Another trick is simply smiling. Imagine that the prospect is standing right in front of you and you're greeting him for the first time. You'd be smiling, wouldn't you? You don't know it, but that smile on your face comes through on the telephone, too. It makes you sound less threatening and more friendly, which makes the prospect more receptive to your message.

If you want proof that these two techniques work, record yourself talking on the phone while sitting and then record the same message standing and smiling. You'll hear the difference.

Don't be distracted from the purpose of each call. You're not selling your company or product, you're selling the client on the value of spending time with you. Enthusiasm is infectious—it can make a sale happen. The more enthusiastic you are, the more the prospect will want to see you.

A note about attitude: Always assume prospects want to see you. If you do, they will.

## Rule 3: Promise A Reward

Make it worthwhile for prospects to spend some time with you. Promise them a reward—and I don't mean a set of steak knives. I'm referring to the *idea* that you've developed especially for them. When you offer to give clients something of value—an idea for improving their business—you're giving them a reason to meet with you. You're paying them for their time.

Remember, if you give the idea away over the phone, there's no reason for an appointment—you've squandered your payment without getting anything for it. You have to keep the idea in the background until the face-to-face meeting.

Tell prospects that the purpose of your call is to arrange a meeting so you can show them your idea—but don't tell them anything about the idea except in very general terms. This serves two purposes. It establishes a reason to meet with you, and appeals to their curiosity.

If you have doubts about the power of curiosity, just think about mystery novels. Does anyone stop reading before they find out "whodunit?" This call works like a mystery novel—it holds prospects' attention.

> Express your regrets, promise to remain in contact, and hang up!

If they press for details, politely point out that you can't *show* them your idea over the phone. You'd like to, but it's not physically possible.

It's OK to talk about one of the benefits of your idea, but never the idea itself. If prospects absolutely insist, give them a morsel of detail, but nothing they can say no to. It's a good idea to plan for this contingency by deciding which tidbit to use as bait *before* you make the call.

What about prospects who absolutely refuse to see you unless you explain your idea in full detail over the phone? Express your regrets, promise to remain in contact, and hang up! Yes, that's right—say goodbye and hang up. You know—and so do prospects— that the only reason they want to hear about the idea now is to say no and avoid a meeting. Why should you pay for something (the appointment) you're not going to receive? Why waste the idea?

There's no point in getting into a tug-of-war with the prospect. You can't possibly win and the longer it goes on, the more likely the prospect is to get aggravated—so cut your losses and move on. I'm not suggesting that you give up on prospects altogether, just that you end *today's* call and try again in a day or two when they might be in a more receptive mood.

If you get the same treatment the next time you call, don't despair. There are other ways to get your idea in front of the prospect. In fact, later on in the book, I'll discuss a tactic that works on people who refuse to give you an appointment—or even take your phone call.

These kinds of prospects are rare. Almost everyone gives you a few minutes if you follow my rules. Remember: Keep that enthusiasm up!

# Rule 4: Guarantee No Obligation

Make sure you observe this fourth rule: Guarantee no obligation to buy. Even prospects' curiosity can be overcome by the fear of being pushed into something. They've seen far too many movie scenes where the salesperson literally sticks a foot in the door to keep the hapless housewife from shutting off a sales pitch. They've read about long-distance service "slamming," where saying no actually authorizes a switch in carriers. Remove that kind of fear.

Make it clear you just want to be heard. Prospects need to realize that agreeing to a meeting is not an obligation to buy. Remove the threat and give prospects the opportunity to let curiosity take over.

# Rule 5: Close Your Appointment

Your primary objective is to set up an appointment, so ask for one! Name a date and time no less than two days, and no more than one week after your call. If prospects can't make your first date, offer two others. Always name the exact date and time yourself. If the second or third dates you offer don't work, most prospects will offer one themselves.

Absolutely never ask "When can we get together?" For one thing, it sounds like your time isn't important enough to be scheduled. It also gives the impression that your calendar is empty—not a

## YOUR 15 MINUTES OF FAME

Never ask for more than 15 minutes of the prospect's time. Fifteen minutes is a small price to pay for an idea—and 15 minutes is easy to manage. The prospect can fit you in between other appointments. Fifteen minutes is a coffee break. Anything longer, and most busy prospects imagine their day eaten away by your presentation. Remember, the prospect's time is valuable.

You can easily complete a standard Creative Selling System proposal in 15 minutes. In fact, if it takes longer than that, it's usually because the prospect is very interested and asks a lot of questions.

good message to send. Prospects get the idea that there's little demand for your product or service. The other problem with posing the question this way is that it makes it much easier for prospects to set an appointment in the distant future—when you'll be less enthused about the pitch, and they'll be more inclined to preempt your meeting for more "pressing" matters. Control the call by asking for a specific date and time in the immediate future.

# MAKING THE CALL

To keep these five rules in mind, it's a good idea to prepare a script for each call. You don't want to sound like a slick salesperson working out of a boiler room, but you also don't want to stumble around looking for the right words. You don't want to forget any important points, so write them down in your own words. For example:

❍ Is this a good time to talk?

❍ I have an idea to give you.

❍ It'll only take 15 minutes to explain.

❍ Can we meet at. . . ? Name the specific time and date.

With a simple outline in front of you, you don't have to exert extra effort trying to remember what to say. The better you know your material, the more you can focus on sharing your enthusiasm.

## Rehearse The Call

It doesn't hurt to rehearse the call a few times before you make it! Rehearse *out loud*. That witty phrase you've had spinning in your mind may not sound quite so impressive when you hear it coming out of your own mouth. You may have accidentally put a tongue twister into your script. The words look fine on paper, but you get tongue-tied when you try to say them. More than anything, rehearsing out loud gives you confidence—the real key to making telephone appointments.

In a well-executed call, the prospect gets two chances to talk. The first one is when you ask "Is this a good time to talk?" The second shouldn't come until you ask your closing question. When you rehearse, try to deliver the four points without pausing. Don't be impolite or rude, but try to get from the idea offer to the closing question without pausing for an answer. You want the prospect to say yes or no to the appointment date, not to the idea. Make sure that's what you ask for when you give them their second turn to talk.

Your call should go something like this:

*You*: "Hello, this is Dave Donelson with SDA. I know you're busy, so I'll just take a minute of your time. Is that OK?"

*The Boss*: "Yeah, but make it quick."

*You*: "I'd like to set up a time when we could meet to discuss a powerful idea that we've developed just for you. If you could spare 15 minutes just to see it, I'll show you how this idea can make you lots of money. Would Wednesday at 10 be convenient for you?"

It's short and to the point—a 30-second phone call asking for a 15-minute meeting. All The Boss has to do is say yes or no.

## Voice Mail

What about voice mail? Navigate the automated operator system (sorry, I can't help you with that one) and get to your prospect's voice-mail box. When leaving your message, just make a couple of simple changes in your script.

First, you obviously don't have to get permission for this phone call. You *do* need to be sure prospects get your name and company right, though, so slow down when you identify yourself. Get right to the point. Offer an idea in return for their time, guarantee no obligation to buy, and ask for the appointment.

> Get right to the point. Offer an idea in return for their time, guarantee no obligation to buy, and ask for the appointment.

The second difference is that you want to offer two dates and times in the first voice mail message. To improve your chances of hitting an open time on the prospect's calendar, offer two meeting times instead of one. Ask for their choice in a return call. Give your phone number—slowly and distinctly—and thank them in advance for the call back.

The one thing to avoid is phone tag. If your first message consists only of your name and number, the odds of getting it returned are slim. If you tell them your company's name or simply say you'd like to set up an appointment, the odds get worse.

To prompt a return call, you must offer a reward—an idea. You should also suggest they leave you a preferred appointment date and time on your voice mail.

Voice mail doesn't have to be just a screening device. More and more professionals are using the tool to improve their productivity. It certainly beats those "while you were out" message slips. Put some meat into your voice mail messages and you'll be surprised at how often they work for you.

# PERSISTENCE COUNTS

There's one overriding key to getting appointments: polite persistence. Your prospects are busy people. They have many demands on their time. They don't always return calls when you want them to. Sometimes they "forget" to return calls. Don't get mad—and don't get even, either. Get focused. If they don't return your first call, wait an appropriate amount of time (anywhere from two hours to a day) and call again. If they don't return your second call, same drill. Same for the third and fourth calls.

Always be polite, especially to the poor folks (including the screener) who have to repeatedly take your messages. It's not their fault the prospect is so busy. The same goes for the messages you leave on the prospect's voice mail. Above all, never, ever complain to anybody about the difficulty of getting through. If you convey even the slightest hint of impatience, their response will be "Who do you think you are?"

If you take nonreturned calls personally, you're doomed to live in perpetual rage. Just relax. There's no magic number of messages to leave before you intensify your effort, but don't drag the process out too long or you'll lose your enthusiasm. Generally speaking, if I've left five messages over a two-week period without getting a return call, I know it's time to call in the heavy artillery.

## Increasing Pressure

But what do you do when the prospect just won't see you? You've called and called, left countless voice mail messages, even "dropped by" unannounced to try to set up an appointment, but The Boss won't give you the time of day. The door is firmly closed. Do you give it up and move on to greener pastures?

Actually, that's a serious option. But before you do, consider the relative value of this prospect and what turning her into a customer could mean to your income and your company's revenues. If you're following the Creative Selling System, every prospect has big potential. You should have confirmed that during your research on the prospect's business. I assume you wouldn't even be calling for an appointment if the prospect wasn't potentially a big customer, so retreating from the closed door isn't an attractive option.

The truly creative seller will embrace the closed door as a challenge to be overcome. And believe me, where there's a will, there really is a way. Let's review some of the obvious (but sometimes forgotten) methods of getting your message to the prospect.

> The truly creative seller will embrace the closed door as a challenge to be overcome.

What's your goal? You're trying to get an appointment, right? Telephone calls haven't worked because she doesn't answer the phone. The prospect also doesn't return phone calls—at least not yours. Have you tried other forms of communication? How about a fax, e-mail, registered letter or telegram? Sometimes the unusual delivery method is enough to break the barrier down. When was the last time your prospect got a telegram?

What about asking someone else to make the phone call? Maybe the prospect will return your sales manager's call, or your company president's. Check to see if one of your company's directors or one of your colleagues is a member of the prospect's country club. Don't let internal politics or your own fear of failure stop you from using these resources. Most of your superiors and peers will view your request as a sign of persistence and a willingness to go the extra mile. As far as career politics go, it never hurts to flatter bosses or seasoned colleagues by asking them to exhibit those powerful skills that raised them above the masses in the first place.

Still no luck? The door is still closed? Up the ante. Don't just send a fax—send flowers. Don't just send flowers—send a brick wrapped up in a note that says you have a "solid idea." Don't just send a brick. . . send a singing telegram delivered by a guy in an ape suit. When you're a truly creative seller, the possibilities are endless.

You have to look on this entire process as a campaign that will take time. Have some fun with it. Pretend you're Richard the Lion-Hearted laying siege to a castle. Every once in a while you launch a couple of stones against the walls with your catapult, but that's mostly just to remind the inhabitants you're not going away. It's the same thing with most prospects. Wear them own by lobbing a few stones at a time.

If none of these methods work and the prospect just won't see you, don't give up—read on. Later in the book I'm going to reveal Dave Donelson's Secret Sure-Fire Door Opener. But before I do, you need to keep the appointment and make that first sales call.

CHAPTER 6

# LIGHTS! CAMERA! SALES!

hy are you paid the big bucks in sales? Because you turn prospects into customers by communicating with them. This chapter will help you do that even better.

Your success as a salesperson depends on your ability to persuasively communicate one-on-one with your prospects. This is no major revelation. What you may not realize, however, is that many of the same skills you were exposed to in Public Speaking 101 are the same ones you use in selling. The techniques your seventh grade English teacher made you use in that stirring oration "Why I Love the Red, White and Blue" are the same ones you use in "Acme Widgets: the Finest Made."

But there's one skill you probably weren't taught in Public Speaking 101: listening.

## LISTENING SKILLS

In my consulting practice, I never talk about the salesperson's speaking ability—I always refer to their communication skills. Communication is a two-party, two-action process. In sales communication, as in other types of interpersonal communication, each person takes turns speaking and listening. Person A talks and Person B listens to what he says. Then Person B replies and Person A listens to the answer. There is a completed communications loop. This happens instinctively, doesn't it?

Wipe that thought from your mind; it doesn't happen instinctively at all. There are countless instances where the communications loop isn't completed. For example:

Your spouse is talking to you about squeezing the toothpaste tube strictly from the bottom, but your mind is on what your best customer was complaining about today, so you don't "hear" a word that's being said. The sound strikes your eardrums and your neural system transmits it to your brain, but it doesn't register because your brain is busy with something else.

Say your sales manager or business partner is going over the pricing strategies for your fall line for at least the tenth time, but you're busy calculating the effects of the new pricing on your commission checks. Your manager is talking and you're hearing, but you are not *listening*. There's a big difference.

Many people think a salesperson's job is to talk. Even worse, many salespeople think that. Salespeople who believe that their job is to *talk* the prospect into submission fail to complete the feedback loop by not listening to what their prospect is saying. And they wonder why their closing ratio is so low.

I'm going to spend a lot of time discussing listening skills throughout this chapter and beyond, so I won't belabor the point.

## HOW'S YOUR DOG?

One of my favorite examples of hearing but not listening occurs when you use that automatic conversation opener "How are you?"

Most of the time, you'll get an automatic answer like "I'm fine. How are you?"

Every once in a while, though, the answer is far from automatic: "I'm terrible. My dog died yesterday, and I'm heartbroken."

But you're still in auto-answer mode, so you come back with "I'm just great, too. I know you're busy, so let's get right into the presentation."

I've done it and so have you. We *think* we're paying attention, but we're not really *listening* at all.

Just remember that more sales are made with your ears (and what's between them) than your mouth.

# The Model Call

There are many kinds of sales calls and presentations: one-on-one across the desk in a private office, in a cubicle with a dozen unseen eavesdroppers on the other side of the dividers, or on the factory floor with machines clanking in the background. Sometimes you may pitch to a group of decision influencers sitting around a conference table or on a conference call. There are specific techniques for each situation, but I'm going to work through the most basic scenario: You're face to face with your prospect in a private office.

Within that context, I'm going to break down the sales call into its individual elements so you can see how they work. I'm going to walk through a typical sales call using a standard Creative Selling System five-page presentation so you can see why I structure it the way I do.

My goal is to equip you for your very first sales call, so excuse me if you've been selling for a while. But this approach is the clearest and easiest to follow. Besides, if you're a new salesperson, or ever had to learn how to sell a new line of products, or represented a new company, you know that one of the hardest things is figuring out what to say on your first few calls. Most salespeople eventually develop their own "patter" through trial and error. But that takes time and can be frustrating. If you follow the techniques I outline, you can make effective sales presentations right away.

# Meeting Needs

As you saw in the first part of this book, the Creative Selling System is based on meeting customers' needs and the creative sales pitch is no different. Start by talking about the prospect's needs and listening to the response. Then offer your product or service as the solution to those needs.

It's as simple as that—except in real life, of course. Despite your best intentions, your mind might drift to huge commissions and sales trips to Vegas. In other words, it's human nature to think about your needs, not the prospect's.

## Prospect Language

The language you use is one reflection of whose needs you're talking about. Your vocabulary reveals knowledge of your industry or your company's products and services, but its specialized terms may not be in the same language the prospect speaks.

One of the biggest dangers of using specialized terms is that not only are they not understood, but they can make prospects feel ignorant. Nobody enjoys that feeling or appreciates the person who gave it to them. Most of the time, prospects won't even let on that they don't understand. After all, who likes to admit their ignorance? In the worst case scenario, you lose the sale because a prospect didn't comprehend what you were trying to say.

### "COME AGAIN?"

Every industry has its own argot, or set of words, acronyms, and codes that serve as verbal shorthand. Some of this jargon is fairly well-known, but most of it isn't.

For example, most people know that a "spot" on television means a short commercial message. But how many know what a "donut" means in TV-language? (It's a commercial message where the beginning and end remain the same from showing to showing but the middle—the hole in the donut—is changed frequently.) Your industry has its own jargon, too.

It's important to identify your specialized terms and make sure your prospect understands them. Be especially careful of acronyms—those collections of initials that are taking over our language.

"We are offering you only Bb+ rated or better NYC GO's, so your 1099 will be very simple."

This may be perfectly clear to a stockbroker or an accountant, but what does it mean to you and me—or the prospect?

That's why you need to know the prospect's specialized language. Sprinkling a few well-chosen, correctly used phrases from The Boss' line of business into your presentation gains you credibility. If you're selling to a car dealer, you should know what an "up" is. Furniture stores carry "case goods" and appliance stores sell "white goods" and sometimes "brown goods." Almost all retailers keep track of their "SKUs." If you're going to sell to prospects in these categories, you need to know their language. Just make sure you use the terms correctly—and don't overdo it.

You will pick up a lot of your prospects' jargon when you do your research. You can also learn a lot by reading trade publications and browsing the Web. Many industry and trade association sites offer a glossary of industry terms that you will find particularly useful.

If you suspect your prospect doesn't understand something, there's nothing wrong with pausing to clear up the confusion. When a prospect gets that quizzical look, stop the pitch and offer to clear up the misunderstanding. Just make sure you blame yourself for the problem by saying something like "I sense that I've failed to make something clear. You look like you have a question." Then give the prospect time and space to ask the question.

## Attention And Interest

Another essential factor to the completion of sales communication is holding the prospect's attention throughout the pitch. That's harder than it sounds, as anyone who has done any public speaking can attest. Holding the listener's attention is one of the hardest tasks a communicator faces, for several reasons.

For one thing, the human brain is programmed to check for distractions—to actually seek them out—while it's listening to you. This involuntary reflex probably dates back to the early days of prehistory when our ancestral prospect's knuckles dragged the ground. As our proto-prospect walked across the savanna he was in constant danger from predators. He had to check out every sound, movement, or scent that came along, just like the deer that raises its head between every bite of grass.

When you are making your presentation, your prospects are constantly tuning in and out of your sales presentation to check for "dangers" lurking about the room. Unlike the deer, however, prospects have a lot of other things on their minds. These subjects pop into their consciousnesses every time they stop listening to what you are saying. Your prospects may be staring right at your face, apparently hanging on your every word. In their heads, however, there's a monologue going on about what their mate said last night at the dinner table, what they are going to have for dinner tonight, how much traffic they can expect to encounter on the commute home, whether their car needs a tuneup, how large the balance on their credit card has become, and on and on. They tune in and out of your presentation the same way they tune in and out the monologue in their head.

You have to continually recapture and hold their interest. Your presentation skills can help you do that.

*Change* is the key to holding interest. The mind attends to changing stimuli. The deer perks up its ears when a twig snaps in the background or the wind sweeps from another direction. Your prospect will tune back into your presentation when something—anything—in your delivery changes.

Work on varying the volume, pitch and tone of your voice. We've all sat through presentations delivered in a monotone and know how deadly boring even the most interesting subject can be if it's delivered in a constant drone.

## MIRROR, MIRROR, ON THE WALL...

A few dos and don'ts about appearance: gum, cigarettes or anything else that goes in your mouth shouldn't be there during a sales call. They not only interfere with your ability to speak clearly, they make you look highly unprofessional. And there's always the possibility that your wad of gum might pop out of your mouth and land on the prospect's desk.

If you're offered coffee or a cold drink, have one if the prospect is having one. Sharing sustenance is a bonding experience, so take advantage of the opportunity. If the prospect isn't partaking, however, you're better off without.

Dress appropriately—in the same manner or slightly better than your prospects. Take note of their degree of formality when you make your reconnaissance visit.

○ Speak louder and softer, emphasizing different points in your presentation with different vocal volumes.

○ Practice speaking in higher and lower pitches—which help convey excitement and intimacy.

○ Work on different tones for different places in your presentation—authoritative, humorous, decisive, inquisitive.

Every time you change your delivery, you get the prospect's attention back on your pitch.

You can also vary the rate, intensity and pacing of your speech. Some people seem to speak at machine-gun rate all the time. They wear their listeners out trying to keep up. Believe it or not, it's almost impossible to speak too *slowly*. The sentence that seems like it's never going to end will probably sound just fine to the listener.

Remember that the adrenaline pumping through your veins while you're making a pitch will speed you up unless you make a conscious effort to control it. The intensity of your presentation can range from conversational to table-pounding, as long as it's appropriate to the points you're trying to emphasize.

> Don't forget to pause. An intentional silence brings a listener back to you every time.

Don't forget to pause. An intentional silence brings a listener back to you every time. It also underscores the preceding point.

Use body language. It's almost impossible to stay enthusiastic and keep a high energy level if you're slouched in a chair. Stand for most of your presentation. Move about the room, even if it's just a few feet. It helps keep the prospect focused on you and what you're saying.

If you have to sit down while you're making your pitch (and you do, most of the time), sit on the middle of the seat and don't let your body touch the back of the chair. Keep your arms away from the armrests so you don't slouch. Sitting erect makes you more energetic.

Good posture gives you better breath control, too. This puts energy into your voice and helps you speak clearly.

You should make lots of gestures whether you're sitting, pacing or standing still. Gestures recapture interest and provide strong nonverbal emphasis to important points. To help free your hands during the pitch, don't fold them in your lap or on the desk—and don't hold a pen or other object. You'll have a tendency to fidget with it.

## Ask Questions

All these techniques help hold prospects' interest during your presentation. The best technique of all, however, is to ask questions. I'm not talking about closing questions, agreement questions or quizzes about your pitch. I'm referring to questions about the prospect's business needs relative to your idea. That's how you learn what the prospect wants to buy.

When you ask a question, your prospect's attention is immediately brought back into your presentation. Questions demonstrate your interest in the prospect's needs and also shape your current and future offerings. Remember, the purpose of the call is to learn as much as you can about the prospect.

Salespeople who don't ask questions are almost always the same ones who use the same canned pitch on everybody. Prospects who sense a canned presentation won't spend much energy listening to it. After all, if the salesperson doesn't care enough to present a custom idea, why should they care enough to listen?

Questions are so important that I format the entire creative selling presentation, both written and oral, around them. The five-page written presentation prompts you to ask a question at the end of four of the five pages. You're encouraged to ask more than that, of course, but if you at least remember to ask a question before you turn every page, you'll keep both the prospect and yourself involved in the pitch.

# THE CREATIVE SELLING PRESENTATION SCRIPT

Let's go through the written presentation page by page and outline a presentation script for you to follow. You may want to refer to the sample written proposal from Chapter 4 as you go along.

You'll notice that the script includes some stage directions. That's because what you do and what the prospect sees are just as important as the words you use.

## Opening The Sale

*Page One (Cover):* Take one copy of the presentation out of your briefcase, but don't just hand it to prospects. Before they even see it, you need to briefly cover three items and ask a question. This is the introduction to your presentation, so keep it as conversational as possible.

In the first sentence, set up the need. In the second, promise to meet the need, which is the prime benefit of your proposed idea. In the third sentence, describe the idea. Finally, ask the prospect a general question to signal it's OK to interrupt your pitch.

Let's use the St. Luke's Hospital presentation as your example. Your opening statements would go something like this:

"We've been studying the health-care market and have observed that St. Luke's is a great institution with a lot of competition." *(The Problem)*

"To help St. Luke's stand out from that competition *(The Benefit)*, we've developed a year-long marketing plan for your consideration."

"We recommend a series of TV messages highlighting the caring nature of St. Luke's as exemplified by the many fine volunteer organizations that help you." *(The Idea)*

> If you at least remember to ask a question before you turn every page, you'll keep both the prospect and yourself involved in the pitch.

"Does that sound interesting?" *(The Question)*

Read that sequence out loud and time yourself. You'll notice that it takes less than 30 seconds to say all four of those sentences and accomplish those tasks. If the introduction takes longer than that, you're spending too much time on it.

In the introduction, tell the prospect what's coming in the presentation so it can be absorbed better. This is very important because people need repetition of key points to truly understand them. One of the best ways to do this is to practice one of the first rules from Public Speaking 101:

"Tell them what you're going to tell them. Tell them. Then tell them what you told them."

Control of the written presentation sheet also comes into play here. Assuming you're sitting across the desk from your prospects (and not in a conference room addressing a group), use only one copy and hold on to it. Don't hand it to prospects! If they reach for it, politely tell them that you'll leave them a copy but you need this one to go through the idea. Then use the written presentation as a visual aid.

The reason for this is simple. You don't want prospects looking for the price while you're trying to explain the benefits. You want to control the pace and timing of as many elements of the call as you can.

You can accomplish the same thing if you have access to a laptop and good presentation software, or with a desktop presentation easel. There are, however, some drawbacks to computer demonstrations. I once flew halfway across the country to make a really snazzy presentation with my laptop. Then the little gremlin that lives inside all computers decided that the presentation wasn't going to run (after three tries in front of the squirming prospect). I had to deliver the pitch a cappella, so to speak. Have you ever known a computer to work exactly how you want it to when you want it to?

I prefer simply holding one copy of the written presentation so the prospects can see it but can't hold or control it. My upside-down reading skills are now second nature.

## Selling The Benefits

*Page 2 (Benefits):* This page has three short bullet points summarizing the benefits your idea will bring to the prospect. Your commentary should cover each of the benefits, rephrasing and repeating each one three times before you move on to the next one. The last thing you do before you turn the page is—you guessed it—ask a question.

Going back to the St. Luke's example, the first bullet point on the benefits page is:

❍ Maintain and enhance the caring reputation the hospital has earned throughout your service area.

You rephrase and repeat this benefit three different times:

1. "Our program is designed to maintain and enhance your caring reputation."

## THE JUJITSU ALTERNATIVE

**B**ut what if you ask a question and the answer is no? What if all your research and brainstorming have pinpointed a need that the prospect can't or won't perceive? If that's the case, take the presentation off the table and start asking questions. Just like in jujitsu, you use prospects' own momentum to move them in the direction you want them to go.

You're there to learn, just as much as you are to sell (it's the first call, remember?), so keep the door open for your next presentation by switching on your prime selling apparatus—your ears. Here are some learning questions to ask:

○ "That's interesting. Could you elaborate on the goals you want to achieve?"

○ "I appreciate your candor. Could you tell me more?"

○ "Let's not waste any of your time on this particular idea, then, since it's designed to reach these specific goals. Tell me what you'd like to accomplish so I can give some thought to another idea."

You need to be prepared for this contingency, but you'll be surprised at how seldom it happens. If you're a conscientious creative seller and do your homework before the meeting, your benefits will match the prospect's needs most of the time. Besides, if you've gotten this far, the prospect wants to hear your idea before passing final judgment.

2. "It's taken years of hard work to build a reputation for delivering warm, responsive care and we want to spread that word to every corner of the market."

3. "St. Luke's is known as the best, and we can demonstrate that very clearly on television."

Remember, repetition sells. After you've presented the other two benefits in the same way, it's time for another question, which might be something like, "Are these goals consistent with your goals?" or "Have we identified some goals you'd like to accomplish?" If the answer to your question is yes, you'll go on with the presentation.

# Selling The Idea

*Page 3 (Your Idea):* Once the benefit question is answered, turn to the idea page and explain how it works. Try to go step by step through the elements of your plan and make sure prospects comprehend each one before moving on to the next one. Here's where you'll start getting questions, so take your time and explain everything in detail.

The very best salespeople paint such a vivid picture of their idea, prospects can almost "see" it taking shape. Keep up your enthusiasm. You've brought in an exciting idea and you want prospects to get excited about it, too. Make them hear bells ringing and cheers rising as the world recognizes the brilliant decision it is to buy your idea. Sell it!

And ask another question before you turn the page.

Prospects know when you're getting ready to ask for the order, so ease the tension by saying something like "I know you're wondering how much this is going to cost, and I'm getting to that next. But first, do you like the idea?" or "No obligation—would you like to do this?"

You have to get a positive response, or there's no point in going on to the proposal page. If your prospect likes the idea, the price hurdle is the only one left. If the prospect doesn't like the idea, the price doesn't matter—it's time to take the proposal off the table and ask some more questions:

○ "What bothers you about it?"

○ "Is there something else you have in mind?"

○ "How can we change this to make it work for you?"

Before I go on, let me point out that you're not asking these questions to identify and answer objections. That shouldn't be your attitude at this or any other point in the presentation. You're simply asking questions to get a clearer understanding of how you can better serve the prospect. You're not trying to argue. If you do, you'll blow your budding relationship.

# Selling The Investment

*Page 4 (Your Proposal):* This is the only page where you're *not* going to ask a question at the end. But you *are* going to carefully review the specifics of what you're selling.

Think of this as a way to anticipate the "Why?" questions and to answer them before they get asked. *Why* you chose this exact selection of widgets. *Why* you're scheduling these particular commercial announcements. *Why* you're asking the prospect to buy these three special services instead of those other three. In short, you're exhibiting your expertise in helping the prospect make the best use of your company's products or services.

You also want to point out how a particular product or feature in your plan delivers a specific benefit you're selling. Your goal at this point isn't to justify the price, it's to demonstrate that your plan works for the prospect.

> Your goal at this point isn't to justify the price, it's to demonstrate that your plan works for the prospect.

This is an important time to keep your ears open. If you've gotten this far, the prospect has some interest in doing business with you. The comments and observations made about your proposal will tell you worlds of information about the prospect's likes and dislikes, hot buttons and turn-offs. You'll need that information to close this sale or open the door to the next one, so *listen*.

## The Moment Of Truth

Now, there it is—right at the bottom of the page, staring prospects in the face—jumping off the paper: the price. You know they see it. They know you know they see it. They also know when you're getting ready to ask for the order—so do it!

In one fluid sentence, state the price, turn the page, restate the prime benefit, and ask for the order.

Don't skip any of these four actions, and do them in this exact sequence. You must turn the page so that the prospect is looking at the benefits, not the price, when you ask for the order. It's a small but vital step. Prospects are much more likely to say yes to buying benefits than they are to spending money. You want them to envision the benefits rather than the draining of their bank account.

The fifth page (the one you turn to) is a repeat of the second page. That's so you don't have to fumble around looking for it when you're going through this sequence.

*Do not pause* at any step in this process, even for breath. This encourages the prospect to comment on the price. When you stop talking, it sends a signal to prospects that it's their turn to start. Prospects almost always start talking about the last item mentioned, which in this case is the price. In my experience, they never say "Gee, that's not very expensive at all."

That's what happens to many salespeople. They actually encourage the prospect to raise a price objection. It's easy to do unless you're prepared to avoid it. You've been encouraging the prospect to talk throughout the pitch. You've solicited their opinion on everything you've said. It's only natural to do the same with the price. But that's the one time you don't want the prospect's opinion.

Besides, you probably won't have to ask for it. Most prospects will offer their opinion on your price whether you want it or not. Don't make it any easier for them. We'll get into handling price (and other) objections in the next chapter. For now, just concentrate on managing your presentation so that the prospect is looking at the benefits page (the last one) when you ask for the order.

Also, make sure you explicitly ask for the order. You'd be surprised at how many salespeople don't. They may *think* they're asking, but they're really not. You need to say and mean just one thing: "Do you want to buy this today?"

The closing sequence for St. Luke's would go something like this:

"Your investment in this program is less than $10,000 per month *(turn to the last page)*, and for that investment you'll have a TV marketing program that further enhances St. Luke's stellar reputation. Would you like to make that investment?"

Read these two sentences out loud without taking a breath. Be especially careful not to pause as you're turning the page. That's the end of your presentation.

It's not the end of the call, of course, because now it's time to be quiet and really listen.

# LISTEN HARD

There are three reasons to keep your mouth shut and your ears open. First, you don't want to miss prospects saying yes. Second, you need to hear their questions, modifications and concerns. Finally, you don't want to talk yourself out of the sale.

The sales adage "He who talks first, loses," is generally true, but not for the reason most people think. You're not engaged in a power struggle with prospects, which is what this adage implies. Salespeople are likely to lose the sale if they talk first, simply because they're not giving prospects a chance to say yes. Give them a chance to speak before you jump in with more information. If you won't shut up and let them talk, they can't give you an order.

While you're hearing what they are saying, be sure to really *listen*—so their words register in your brain. It's an easy time to get distracted. You've been focused on making your presentation up until this point, but now your mind has a chance to seek other stimuli. Don't let it. Listen to the comments the prospect is making about your idea.

Your silence also keeps you from talking yourself out of the order. It's a tremendous temptation to offer just one more tidbit of information, one more reason the prospect should buy, one more point. But don't do it. You're just as likely to bring up a new objection as you are to present a new reason to buy.

# REHEARSAL

So, are you ready to go out there and sell? Not just yet. First you need to work on your stagecraft. Making a sales presentation is a lot like acting out a drama—you have to deliver lines and follow stage directions. Good actors communicate emotions to their audience—the same is true for you and prospects. But you can't do any of these things if you don't know your role. That's why you need to rehearse.

There are lots of effective ways to rehearse. Get a friend or co-worker to play the prospect. If you can get past the side issues, you can even ask your sales manager to help out.

If you want to work alone, pitch yourself. Sit in front of a mirror while you make your presentation. If you have a video camera or a tape recorder, use these tools as well.

Just make sure to practice as if it's real—out loud, with props, and in costume. Running through your lines silently doesn't help you work on tone, speech rate, intensity, gestures and other techniques that will make your performance an award-winner.

The goal of rehearsal is to make you more confident. If you know your lines, you can concentrate on your delivery instead of what you're supposed to say next. If you've rehearsed your questions, they won't sound forced or artificial—and you'll be able to listen to the answers instead of worrying about your lines.

The repetition of your idea will also make you more confident of its value to the prospect. Your enthusiasm will increase with each practice session until you'll be a dynamo in front of the prospect. Remember, enthusiasm is contagious—and you want your prospect to catch it from you.

There are two parts of the script that I suggest memorizing: the opening sequence and the closing. It's important at both of these points to sound confident, to be in total control, and to say the lines smoothly. The best way is to actually memorize the lines.

# STAGE FRIGHT

Do you suffer from stage fright? I hope so! You'll be a more effective seller if you do.

I've done thousands of sales presentations, speeches, seminars, and live radio and TV appearances—and I still get butterflies in

## MAKE STAGE FRIGHT YOUR FRIEND

There is a little secret to controlling the intensity of your stage fright symptoms. As you're waiting in the lobby before your presentation or just before you get out of your car to see your prospect, take the edge off by doing some simple exercises. Press your palms together—hard—for 30 seconds. Grip your steering wheel or the arms of your chair as hard as you can for another half minute. This will burn off some of that excess adrenaline in your system while leaving you the energy you need to convey enthusiasm.

Now take a couple of long, deep breaths, using your diaphragm to completely fill your lungs. Slowly let out each breath to a count of 10. This steadies your voice for a powerful opening statement.

Your stage fright has now become a reservoir of energy. You'll focus better on the prospect, and your presentation will be more intense and powerful.

my stomach and sweaty palms. Every good speaker has similar reactions.

Most speakers welcome them because they are signs that our energy level is going to be high. In fact, if I don't have an attack of stage fright before I speak, I know I'm not focused on my presentation and something's distracting me. The same is true before every sales presentation—I *want* the extra energy that comes from an attack of stage fright.

Stage fright is your friend—all you have to do is control it. The first step is to recognize the cause—a small adrenaline rush prompting a fight or flight response to a perceived danger. The next step is to make a conscious decision to fight rather than take flight. You know you've made the right choice when your concentration turns away from yourself and toward the prospect. You replace your fear with intense concentration.

This change energizes your presentation—using the adrenaline rush to your advantage. You've made stage fright your friend.

Now, have you learned your lines? Rehearsed your role? If so, it's time to make your presentation.

# CHAPTER 7

# VARIATIONS
# ON THE THEME

o, how have your calls gone so far? I hope you've made a bunch of creative selling presentations and closed every one of them. I expect you've encountered a situation or two where your script didn't apply. Selling is just like playing chess—the rules are the same every time but no two games are alike. It's a good thing, too, since we'd get bored pretty quickly if the games started repeating themselves.

The sales call script covers the basic strategy and tactics you'll need for the majority of calls. Those are one-on-one "face" calls that consist of a meeting between you and the decision maker. There are a few other types of calls and situations, however, where some modifications to the script are necessary. These are group presentations, team calls, and getting behind closed doors.

## GROUP PRESENTATIONS

In a group presentation, you pitch an idea to more than one person. It may be the prospect and her assistant, a committee of decision makers and decision influencers, or even a board of directors. When you make a group presentation, you work in a different room setup, ranging from chairs pulled around the prospect's desk to a room with a large conference table. You might even make your pitch to a large group in an auditorium, complete with podium and sound system.

The basic differences between a group presentation and a one-on-one call are the distribution and control of your written materials, and the dynamics of large group meetings. It's important to remember that all the other factors remain the same. Your goal is still to gather information about the prospect, and you still follow the five-page presentation format, asking questions at the end of each page. Your stage presence and enthusiasm are even more important when pitching a group, as is your ability to gain their attention and hold their interest.

## Handling Materials

Handling your written materials is actually easier when you work with a group. To control the pace of the presentation, the best tactic is to hand out one page of the presentation at a time. In a smaller room of participants, you can easily handle this yourself—provided you can walk and talk at the same time.

With a larger group, you may need assistance, which the group members can provide. If you don't have a helper with you, just ask the people nearest to you to "take one and pass them on." Your goal is for everyone in the group to get a copy, but you don't want anyone reading a page until you're ready to talk about it.

## Visual Aids

Larger group presentations often call for visual aids, which both embellish and complicate your presentation. Most of the advice you need deals with preventing the problems inherent in using these tools. Whether you're using foamboard flip cards or a laptop with presentation software, be sure you know how to use the medium and have rehearsed with it.

Try to find out just how large the room is and how many participants you have. This helps determine what kind of visual aids you might want to use. You may not want 24- x 30-inch flip cards for a group of four—unless they're going to be seated at the opposite end of a 20-foot table.

Never count on the prospect to provide equipment. There's nothing worse than trying to connect your laptop to the prospect's projector only to discover that you need an adapter neither one of you has. Whether you're going high-tech or low-tech, bring every single

# LIKE A BOY SCOUT, BE PREPARED

**Pre-Meeting Information Checklist**

❏ How many people will attend?

❏ How large is the room?

❏ Is the seating auditorium or conference style?

❏ Can the lighting be dimmed selectively?

❏ Is there a sound system?

❏ Is there a screen or matte-finish white wall?

❏ Can I plug in my equipment?

❏ Have I tested *every* piece of equipment?

❏ Have I looked at *every* slide or transparency?

❏ Have I viewed the *entire* laptop presentation?

❏ Has *someone else* proofread all visuals?

**Low-Tech Equipment Checklist**

❏ Flip cards

❏ Presentation easel

❏ Pointer

❏ Whiteboard

❏ Markers and eraser

**Medium-Tech Equipment Checklist**

❏ Overhead projector

❏ Slide projector

❏ Spare bulb(s)

❏ Glass cleaner and paper towels

❏ Transparencies

❏ Slide trays

❏ Markers

❏ Pointer

❏ Screen

❏ Extension cord

❏ Grounded plug adapter

**High-Tech Equipment Checklist**

❏ Laptop

❏ Presentation shortcut

❏ Spare battery

❏ Extension cord

❏ Grounded plug adapter

❏ Multiple outlet adapter

❏ NTSC converter

❏ Portable speakers

❏ Projector

❏ Spare bulb(s)

❏ Cables

❏ Screen

❏ Laser pointer

**Universal Checklist**

❏ Proposal copies

❏ Wireless microphone system

❏ Business cards

item you could possibly need. This includes everything from extension cords and grounded-outlet adapters to monitors and projectors.

This "Be Prepared" rule doesn't just apply to high-tech presentations, either. If you need an easel for your flip cards, bring one. I guarantee that if you don't, the prospect's won't work or someone in another department will have borrowed it just before you arrived.

> It's better to make a solid low-tech impression than a distracting high-tech one.

Set up your visual aids before the group gathers in the room. I would rather skip the visual aids completely than stumble through a pitch while I'm fumbling with a folder of transparencies or dealing with a "General Protection Page Fault" on my laptop. In fact, if you can't access the meeting room before the group gathers, play it safe and don't bother with the visual aids. It's better to make a solid low-tech impression than a distracting high-tech one.

If you're going the low-tech route, make sure your easel is sturdy enough to stand up while you're changing cards. If you're using a laptop, set up your software so that you don't have to click through several screens to get to your presentation. I've found it helpful to create a Windows shortcut to the presentation I'm making right on my opening screen. That way, all I have to do is click on it to start the show. In either case, check the view from the back of the room to be sure everyone can read your material.

No matter what medium you use, design your visual aids like your written presentation. Make each slide or card simple, clear, and to the point. You'll want to follow the same five-page written presentation format, although you may need to break the idea page and proposal page into more than one slide for clarity. Also, convert bodies of text to bullet points. If you really want to do your slide presentations right, get a good tutorial.

## Group Dynamics

The dynamics of group presentations can be interesting, to say the least. This is a sales presentation, not a floor show, so you'll want to encourage questions and comments. In fact, you'll want to ask some questions of your own, just like you would if you were meeting with the prospect one-on-one.

Your questions can either be thrown out to the group as a whole or addressed to one person, depending on which is more appropriate. You will find that agreement questions such as "Do you like this idea?" don't work very well in a group setting. There's too much danger of the group splitting into factions or a particularly outspoken member shooting you down before you get into your presentation.

Information questions such as "Who is your biggest competitor?" work well. Many times, they spark an inter-group discussion, which is a great time to listen closely and learn a lot. Watch the group dynamics to learn who the leaders are. Obviously, you'll want to listen to what they say about their business, their market, and their competitors as well as what they say about your idea, your company and your competitors.

You should welcome questions or comments that come from the group, even when they break up the flow of your presentation. If the question is one you don't want to answer yet, it's perfectly acceptable to say that you're going to cover that subject in a minute. Just make sure you *do* cover it before you end your presentation. If it's a question about your proposal that indicates the listener doesn't understand something, take the time to make it clear. If one person didn't get it, there are probably others who missed it, too.

## Group Dangers

On very rare occasions, a group presentation will turn ugly. No matter what happens, keep your cool. If you get a hostile question or comment, thank the person for sharing their thoughts with you, then deal with it just like you would handle an objection (which I'll cover in the next chapter). If the whole room starts twitching in their seats, stop your pitch and ask them if you've said something wrong, then correct your misstatement.

The most common problem you'll face with groups isn't hostility, it's keeping them on the track you want them to follow. It seems like every group has a leader or a loudmouth (sometimes it's the same person) who wants to comment on every point you make, and everything everyone else says, too. Don't take it personally. This person probably acts the same way every time this group gets together. In fact, you can usually identify these people before they open their mouths. The rest of the crowd starts rolling their eyes the first time they see the loudmouth's hand go up.

I wish I had a magic incantation for you to use in this situation, but I've never heard one. All you can do is stay pleasant and polite, not hesitating to change the subject back to your presentation before the loudmouth can ask a follow-up question. Resist the temptation to put him in his place the way a stand-up comic does a heckler in a nightclub. Just grin and bear it and try not to lose your place in your pitch. Actually, the sympathy the rest of the group feels for you might work in your favor

Another unpleasant situation is the meeting that degenerates into the dreaded "Who Can Top Who?" routine. When the war stories start, it seems like everyone in the room has to contribute one. Each one has to be more horrible than the last one, of course. If the negative energy goes unchecked, you end up with an ugly mob on your hands.

Once again, the best tactic is to jump in before the momentum builds. Interrupt after the second story. Don't let the third one even get started. Give a polite "That's very interesting" and get back into your presentation. If you're really good, you'll be able to relate the benefits of your proposal to the problem that sparked the first story.

Group presentations are actually fun to give. You get to practice your craft in a slightly different way from the normal routine and you have the opportunity to use all your persuasive skills and stage-craft. Most group presentations involve prospects with large potential, so there's a lot riding on the effectiveness of your presentation.

# TEAM PRESENTATIONS

The team call is when two or more people from your company pitch a single prospect. It's not exactly the reverse of a group presentation, but it's close. Depending on whether your sales manager or business partner is involved or not, the purpose of the double team call can be twofold: to help you make the sale and/or to improve your performance on subsequent calls. I'm going to deal with the first scenario. You have to cope with the second one on your own for now.

Team calls make prospects feel less like the target of a sales shark and more like the object of the company's affections. They get the strong message that the seller's company wants to work with them to solve their problems. They're usually flattered that their business is so important, the selling company is devoting an entire team to getting and handling it.

The interpersonal dynamics of a team call are very different from those of a group presentation. This is because you need to manage your team members' behavior as well as the prospect's.

# Team Members

Anyone in your company can be a part of the pitch team. Other salespeople, engineers, the CEO, even a purchasing agent or shipping clerk can contribute to the sales presentation. Their involvement can make the sales call extremely effective.

One of the most difficult dynamics is when your boss is the other half of your tag team. His or her presence raises all kinds of questions. What's he there for? Can you get any brownie points on the call? Is she going to eyeball your every move? It's a tough situation.

The best strategy is to try to concentrate on impressing your prospect, not your boss. You'll have plenty of opportunities to kiss up to the boss, but you may only have one chance to close this particular prospect. Hopefully, your boss will understand.

# Team Call Preparation

Preparation for the team call is essential. You should each know your roles before you begin the presentation. Even if you've done

## SING FROM THE SAME PAGE

To keep your team call focused on results, make sure everyone on the team understands these points about the upcoming call:

○ What are we trying to do?

○ If this call is successful, what will happen?

○ Who are the key players?

○ What happened on the last call?

○ What are we going to ask them to do?

○ Why should they do it?

The choir always sounds better when they're all singing the same song.

the presentation together many times, rehearse it before you go into the meeting. This means *everyone* on the team, including your company's CEO. And the practice must be a full dress rehearsal complete with the actual props you're going to use.

In addition to the pitch, you should also rehearse the answers to potential questions and objections. It's important to know who will answer which question, so there's no fumbling when it arises. If the prospect asks you about delivery dates, you don't want a long, awkward pause followed by three people giving three different answers all at once. You also don't want your team leader to hand off a question to someone who's not expecting it.

## A $6 Million Mistake

One of my most embarrassing moments occurred during a team presentation. It happened because we had not rehearsed with the actual materials we were going to use. There were four of us making a pitch that we had done many times together. Our presentations usually involved the top decision makers and were quite lengthy and detailed. We typically used a lot of boilerplate material, but the key points were always customized for each prospect.

The climax of the pitch came when I presented our revenue projections for the prospect. I typically jumped into that page like a preacher at a revival, giving it everything I had. On this occasion, when I turned the page I saw the headings of the columns of figures carried not this prospect's name, but the name of the company we pitched the week before. The figures were correct, but they looked like they belonged to another company.

We all saw the mistake at the same time and everyone in the room was embarrassed, including the prospect. But the damage had been done. This little mistake completely undermined the "personal attention to each client" benefit that was our primary selling point. It cost us a $6 million client. The material had been proofread by three people, including me. But we hadn't used the actual materials in our rehearsal the night before. I still believe we would have caught the mistake if we had followed that simple rule.

You also need to organize your visual aids under the management of one team member. We've all seen blooper videos where three out-fielders collide under the same fly ball. You don't want to drop the ball in front of a room full of prospects, so make sure each piece of equipment and each handout is one person's responsibility. Your handouts should be managed the same way they are in a group presentation—the team member responsible for them passes them out with the order and flow you want.

## Team Call Leadership

While I'm on the subject of assigning responsibility, let's talk about leadership. Each team, even if it consists of only two members, should have a leader. Prospects usually address questions to the team leader. Generally, the leader opens the presentation and asks the closing question. If there is any question about who's going to be the leader on your team, settle it before you go into the presentation.

But don't let the leader look like the Grand Pooh-bah attended by his retinue. If the leader delegates all the menial tasks like handing out materials to the "lackeys" on the team, the prospect is liable to sense a power display and react negatively. Eliminate this problem before it arises and make sure the leader is perceived as a *member* of the team, not its monarch.

Also make sure that every team member participates in the presentation. Each person should have a speaking role of some sort, preferably related to their role in the seller's plan. You don't want the prospect wondering why that guy in the corner isn't saying anything. The Metropolitan Opera may need spear carriers, but your sales team doesn't.

Immediately after the call, you should each jot down some notes on what you learned about the prospect, what steps need to be taken to close the sale (if necessary), and how to make the next presentation better. Then compare notes. Complete this process before critiquing individual performances.

# THE CLOSED DOOR

There's one more contingency to discuss: the closed door. You can't get your foot in it because prospects won't even crack it open.

Your phone calls are never returned. Your singing telegrams are heard by a secretary. You've tried all the methods, but this door is closed, locked, and sealed. How do you get your presentation in front of someone who won't see you?

Have no fear. There's a tactic that I guarantee will work *every time you use it*. This technique will require some extra work on your part, but it's a foolproof way to compel your prospect to listen to your presentation.

# Dave Donelson's Secret Sure-Fire Door Opener

I personally guarantee that your prospect will view your presentation if you record it on an unlabeled videotape, put it in a plain brown wrapper, and send it addressed to him personally at his home.

It's human nature—curiosity gets you every time.

I stumbled on this tactic while trying to work around a problem with one of my clients. We were working on a different problem when we found this key to the closed door. When I saw results the first time, I knew we had a powerful tool and subsequent trials proved it.

My client had a simple problem. She wanted to pitch an advertising campaign for a local store to a prospect with headquarters several hundred miles away, but her boss wouldn't approve the travel expense because the prospect wasn't a current customer. In the manager's defense, all the other salespeople in the company also failed to sell this prospect, so why spend money on a lost cause?

My client borrowed a home video camera from a friend and put her pitch on tape. The presentation wasn't anything fancy, just the same pitch she would make if she were sitting across the desk from the prospect. She sent it to the prospect, her phone rang about a week later, and she got the order without ever meeting the actual decision-maker face to face.

Why does this technique work? One reason is because it's so different from what the great crowd of "normal" salespeople do. Prospects are besieged by salespeople, all clamoring for a few minutes of time. They send presentation folders, brochures and personal letters with proposals. They come armed with identical laptops and presentation software—and they all tend to look and sound alike.

Your videotape is just another selling medium—the difference is that your version has obviously been prepared just for this particular prospect at some considerable effort. It demonstrates the creative seller's willingness to work hard for the business.

Also, a video presentation is the next best thing to a personal presentation. Prospects can see the steadiness in your eyes, hear the sincerity in your voice, and get caught up in your enthusiasm for the idea. You just can't do those things in a letter.

If you use this technique, be sure to execute the entire plan exactly as I presented it. Don't send a cover letter. Don't even leave a return address on the package or a label on the tape, and under no circumstances send a copy of your written proposal along with the tape. The curiosity factor is lost if the prospect suspects what the tape is about.

Send the tape to the prospect's home if you can. It will receive more attention there than if it lands in the office in-box with the daily junk mail. Besides, the prospect is much more likely to have a VCR at home than at work. To get a home address, start with the telephone book white pages. If you can't find it there, ask the screen-

## YOU'VE GOT NOTHING TO LOSE

**W**henever I advise a client to use the videotape technique, negatives immediately start rushing through their brains. There's a simple positive answer to every one of them:

○ **"I don't have a camera."** Buy one, rent one or borrow one.

○ **"I'm not a TV star."** Don't try to be—just make your presentation as if the camera were your prospect.

○ **"I'll feel silly."** If you're embarrassed about selling, get a new career.

○ **"It won't look professional."** Don't try to film "Gone with the Wind," just sit comfortably in front of the camera and talk.

○ **"He may not have a VCR."** If he's one of the less than 5 percent of Americans who don't, he'll find one.

If you're going to be a creative seller, you've got to take a chance every once in awhile. Work outside the box, as they say. Try something different; you might like it. Besides, what have you got to lose—the prospect won't even see you, right?

er (you never know until you try). If you can't find the prospect's home address, go ahead and send it to the office.

## The Equipment

So how do you go about this? Using the mystery videotape tactic requires some extra work on your part, but it's not as complicated as it sounds.

Borrow or rent a camera that handles full-sized VHS videocassettes. The kind that use a small cassette with an adapter or a Super 8 style cartridge won't work because you need the end product to be compatible with your prospect's home VCR.

### THE BORED DIRECTORS

After I saw the success of the videotape tactic the first time, I started recommending it all over the country. One of my favorite success stories is about a rookie salesperson who used the mystery videotape tactic to open the door to a chain of tire dealerships. The president of the chain wouldn't see her. He kept giving her the lame excuse that "those decisions are made by the managers' board" and refused to let her make her pitch at a board meeting.

So this rookie salesperson who didn't know any better put her pitch on tape and sent a copy of it to the president and to the manager of every store in the chain. She didn't know which ones were on the board, so she sent it to all of them. She made sure the tapes arrived the day before the next scheduled board meeting. And the first words on her tape were "We know you have a lot of important matters to consider at your board meeting, but we hope you'll take 15 minutes to listen to this idea to increase your store sales."

She knew that the message got through because her phone rang the afternoon of the board meeting. It was the president asking her to meet with him to discuss a contract for her proposal. And that account turned out to be one of her company's largest within just a few months—after the door got opened.

A camera with a built-in microphone and light is easier to use. You'll also need a tripod, even if you have someone else operate the camera. You're not producing a major motion picture, but you don't want it to look like the tape of your kid's birthday party, either.

The tape cartridge should not be the standard two-hour cheapie you pick up at the supermarket (although it can be if that's your only alternative). Most electronics stores will sell 30-minute cassettes with a higher grade of tape for about the same price. Don't skimp on the tape quality unless you can't find the best.

Now write your script, which should mirror the presentation you'd make in person. If you feel comfortable enough, ad-lib the pitch like you would on a face-to-face call. You can even work from notes or the written presentation if you are confident of your presentation skills. Doing it this way makes it more natural and, therefore, more effective—and one of the great advantages of videotape is that you can do it over if you make a mistake.

If you're a little camera shy, hand print "idiot cards" and have a friend hold them for you—out of the camera's view, of course.

The "set" for your little production should be as simple as possible. In fact, all you really need is a quiet place with a neutral background. You're only going to have one "shot" for the whole tape: a medium close-up of your head and shoulders. Set up the camera on the tripod for that shot. Check the lighting and sound levels according to the camera's instructions.

# The Production

Now roll the tape. The great thing about videotape is that you can do it over and over again until you get it right—and it doesn't cost you any extra. You can play it back instantly to see how you did. Make every run-through a dress rehearsal with the tape rolling. You'll be surprised at how few "takes" you need to get a finished product.

It's a good idea to ask a friend to help you by starting and stopping the recording, managing the "idiot cards," and giving you a face to talk to. If you need to go solo, look for a camera with remote controls.

Don't overreach your capabilities. Don't try to present the evening news with graphics, multiple camera angles, digital video effects, etc. Unless you have a multimillion-dollar production facility and staff at your disposal, you're not going to be able to approach that quality. All you want is a glitch-free one-way conversation on tape.

You *can* increase the quality of your videotape if you want to invest a little more cash in it. There are video production facilities complete with crews available for rent in most cities. Many quick print services have video conferencing facilities that can also be used to make a tape. If you live in a small town with a local TV station, check with them. Your investment can start at a few hundred dollars and go up from there, so carefully consider the options. Remember, this show will only be seen once by one viewer—it's not going to go into syndicated reruns.

## Your videotape presentation may have a surprising shelf life.

Actually, that last sentence isn't entirely correct. Your videotape presentation may have a surprising shelf life. One of the most incredible experiences with this technique I ever witnessed happened to another one of my clients.

This salesperson was trying to sell a sales promotion campaign to a very hard-to-reach prospect. This wasn't a stereotypical prospect, but was actually an elderly farmer who started a potato-chip business on the side. Like many such entrepreneurs he started small, producing a few bags for friends, then for local stores, slowly expanding his capacity and distribution as demand warranted. My client identified him as a good prospect for his sales promotion services and dreamed up a great campaign to sell him.

As you might have guessed, the farmer wouldn't see him— wouldn't return his calls, respond to his letters—you know the routine. So the salesperson put his pitch on tape and sent it to the farmer, expecting a quick response.

Except it didn't happen. Nothing. No response of any kind. He knew the tape was delivered because he had the FedEx receipt. But the farmer didn't even acknowledge receiving it and still wouldn't return phone calls. When the salesperson told me about it, we both just wrote it off to "win some, lose some."

A full year later we were proved wrong. That's when the salesperson received a phone call from a man who identified himself as the farmer's son. He said, "Dad retired last year, and I took over the potato chip business. I found this tape in his desk without any label on it and took it home to see what it was. The reason I'm calling is to see if we can still get in on that sales promotion you were trying to sell Dad?"

There's no such thing as a closed door that can't be opened.

# CHAPTER 8

# LEAPING TALL OBJECTIONS

ow do you avoid debates and arguments with your customers? How do you manage objections? In short, how do you win a sale?

The classic misguided image of the way a sale is won is of a salesperson glibly presenting the reasons customers should buy the product, overcoming the objections with snappy comebacks, then closing the sale with verbal maneuvers so slick and smooth, customers never even know they bought something. That may be the way you sell aluminum siding to the dimwitted, but it's not the way you sell anything to a businessperson.

My approach to managing objections is very different from the traditional one. I don't believe you win sales by winning arguments—and that's what "overcoming objections" really is—winning an argument.

## OBJECTION DEFINED

What is an "objection?" In the broadest sense, an objection is any obstacle that prevents prospects from buying your proposal. They may believe your product is inferior to your competitor's, for example, or that they don't need what you are selling. The reality may be different, but the prospect's perception is what matters.

Prospects may also tell you the price is too high or that your proposal includes some feature they don't want. This maneuver is just a form of negotiation designed to get you to change your proposal.

Many times, prospects object—or throw up an obstacle to buying—simply because it's their job. Prospects in business-to-business sales are professional buyers, even if their title isn't "purchasing manager." Part of a good buyer's job is to throw up obstacles to test the product and the salesperson's ability to deliver it. They will also test the bottom of your pricing and the top of your product's value. It's a little game they play.

Some of these obstacles are real, and some are not. What you need is a way to identify which are which and a strategy to deal with each kind of obstacle.

## Your Attitude

The Creative Selling System way to deal with objections is to become an ally to your customers, not an adversary. You're not going to prove them wrong for refusing to buy your product; you're going to create a way they *can* buy it. You're not going to demonstrate their ignorance; you're going to educate them. You're not going to overcome their objections; you're going to answer their questions. Above all, you're not going to win the argument; you're going to win the sale. It's a different attitude.

This creative selling attitude is designed to build solid, long-term customer relationships, not make an individual sale. You'll be surprised how many individual sales occur when you adopt this attitude.

# HANDLING OBJECTIONS

The first key to creatively managing objections is to step around them. Don't fight the objection; ignore it. The second is to use the objection to close the sale. It's sort of a jujitsu approach to dealing with objections—you use their own weight and momentum to further your goals.

## Step 1: Listen

What a surprise. The first step in handling an objection is to *listen* to the prospect. Listen to what they say and how they say it. Give

## IS YOUR GLASS HALF FULL?

**D**o you believe that the prospect will buy if you remove all objections? If you do, you're a negative seller. Salespeople who think objections are the reason sales don't occur are pessimists. They start the sales call with an assumption that the prospect has objections and go in looking for a fight. It's basically a negative outlook.

It's also pretty short-sighted. I've seen plenty of prospects still refuse to buy after all their objections have been answered and all obstacles removed. Why? Because they don't have a *positive* reason to buy.

People don't buy just because they can; they buy because they want to. If you want to be a positive seller—a truly *creative* seller—approach each prospect with the attitude that you're going to keep adding reasons to buy until the sale occurs. Your closing ratio will go up tremendously.

them time to talk. Make sure you hear what the prospect is saying and react accordingly.

You need to *really listen*. The next time you encounter an objection, step back and observe yourself in action. When the prospect is talking, are you processing the information, or are you preparing your reply? Are you listening or getting ready to talk? These are two mutually exclusive activities.

Salespeople who overcome objections are invariably preparing their comeback while the prospect is talking. They practice what every good adversary practices—they are prepared. When the prospect starts throwing that punch at them, they strike back. They truly believe that in sales, the best defense is a good offense. It's the old "Ready—Fire—Aim."

This is one of the most common causes of failure to close. More often than not, the salesperson who's not truly listening will answer an objection that doesn't exist! Not only does this salesperson not deal with the real obstacles, he or she may be planting some new ones.

I've seen it happen thousands of times in the field and even captured it on videotape in my training seminars. Don't let it happen to you. Make sure you listen to what the prospect is saying before you

## CAPTURED ON TAPE

One of the most helpful learning techniques (or tortures) I use when training is videotaped role-playing. In one of my basic courses, I have the "prospect" make a comment designed to trap the "salesperson" who isn't listening into answering an objection that doesn't exist. It's kind of sneaky, but it teaches the lesson very well.

In my little drama, the "prospect" waits until the salesperson asks for the order, then makes the comment "Gee, this is a lot of money." That's all. No explanation or other comments. Just those words. You'll notice that the prospect doesn't say "It's too much money," or "I'm not going to pay this," or anything else judgmental or argumentative. They just make an observation.

Invariably, the salesperson will launch into their favorite answer to the ever-popular price objection and raise all sorts of issues that the prospect never even mentioned. They deftly demonstrate the relationship between price and value. They reduce their price to absurdity by calculating the cost per hour of their annual contract. They start calculating return on investment. They bad-mouth their competitor's product, service and management.

Believe it or not, salespeople in my training sessions have been known to do this even when they've been forewarned that it was going to happen! When I play the tape back for the critique, many salespeople have to watch it two or three times before they actually *hear* what the prospect says.

deal with the objection—you might just learn that you don't have to deal with anything at all.

# Step 2: Restate

To make sure you're hearing what the prospect is saying (and for a couple of other pretty good reasons), restate the objection after the prospect stops talking.

You accomplish several things when you restate the objection.

First, you make sure you've got it right—that you understand what they said. It gives the prospect a chance to correct your understanding before you do any damage by answering the wrong objection.

Second, it gives you a little time to think about what your next action should be. Is this a question or an objection? Is it sincere or a smoke screen? Should you correct a misperception? Is there some information that the prospect missed or that you forgot to provide? You need some time to consider these things and restating the objection gives you that time.

It also gives prospects time to reconsider the objection. Have you ever made a statement, then realized how wrong it was when someone repeated it back to you? Prospects may have the same reaction when they hear their own words. They may even withdraw the statement and remove the obstacle. It happens often enough to make it worth trying.

> The biggest reason for restating the objection is that you get a chance to soften it—to put it into your own words so you can deal with it on your own terms.

But the biggest reason for restating the objection is that you get a chance to soften it—to put it into your own words so you can deal with it on your own terms.

Salespeople repeatedly encounter the same objections, which is both a blessing and a curse. The curse is that you start giving the same answers as soon as you hear the prospect raise a common objection. That's what happens in my videotaped role-play exercise (see "Captured on Tape" on page 108).

The blessing is that you have an opportunity to prepare your answers in advance since you generally know what objections you're going to hear. I suggest that, in addition to coming up with stock arguments for stock objections, you develop some standard restatements of those objections. That will make the softening process much easier—and your management of the objections go more smoothly.

It's not a bad idea to confirm your restatement, depending on the flow of the conversation. This can be as simple as saying "Is that what you mean?" or "Did I understand you correctly?" along with the restatement. This buys you a little more time and helps keep the tone of the exchange nonargumentative.

That's what this is all about. Restating the objection reinforces your position as the prospects' ally, not their adversary. You're not only listening to what they say, you're making sure you understand it. It sets a tone of agreement instead of a tone of argument.

## Step 3: Agree

The next step expands the good feelings because you essentially agree with the objection.

This makes prospects feel good. You've told them how perceptive they are to have found a weakness in your idea. You've congratulated them on seeing through to the heart of the matter. You've praised them for helping you analyze the situation correctly—and you do all this by saying anything but "You're wrong."

> The next step expands the good feelings because you essentially agree with the objection.

Agreeing with the objection doesn't mean that you give up and walk out. It just means you're ready to deal with the substance of the objection in a nonconfrontational manner.

There are several alternative routes you can take at this point. Your first choice should always be to just ignore the objection and go on with your presentation. You've listened to and acknowledged the prospect's perception, so get on with your pitch.

This isn't as crazy as it sounds because it's the best way to find out if the objection is just a smoke screen. If it's a real obstacle, it will come up again when you ask for the order. If it's not, it'll just go away—and this happens more often than not. Either way, you haven't lost any ground.

If you've listened carefully, you may learn that you're dealing with a lack of information or a misperception rather than an objection. Obviously, you don't want to ignore these. Clear them up right away with a short statement of the facts. Apologize for confusing the point in question, then correct the error.

Remember, you're not doing this because the prospect is too stupid to understand you but because you're too excited about the proposal to get everything out clearly. It's an attitude thing.

Once you've agreed with the prospect, you have to get back into the flow of your presentation. The best way to jump-start the pitch is to go back to the benefits page of the proposal. It never hurts to repeat them, and they're good neutral ground to revisit since the prospect has already agreed with them. Just touch on them lightly and then get on with the other points you're making.

This technique—going back to the benefits—is also a good one to use with other types of interruptions, such as a phone call the prospect takes in the middle of your meeting.

## Step 4: Close

As soon as you can, take the final step in managing an objection—close the sale. This may seem a little aggressive, but it's actually a natural extension of the conversation you're having with the prospect. You've just completed the final step in the closing process, which is reviewing the benefits. You've agreed on some issues, right? So why not extend that agreement to the proposal itself?

---

### TAKE TWO

Let's rewind the tape and start over from the point where the prospect baits the trap in the videotaped role-play. You'll see how the four steps work.

○ The prospect says "Gee, this is a lot of money."

○ The wary salesperson waits a beat to see if there's more to come out of the prospect's mouth. That's the listening step.

○ Then come the next three steps: "Yes, this is a substantial investment. Would you like to make it today?"

It's simple. It's nonargumentative. You're both saying the same thing, only your words sound more positive. You've told the prospect he's a genius for recognizing the size of the purchase—and now that you've cleared up the little matter of the price, you ask for the order.

About the only time you can't close the sale on an objection is if you haven't covered the price. Even then, you can "close in principle" by phrasing your question conditionally: "Assuming we agree on the size of your investment, would you like to execute this plan?"

You'll have to judge whether and how to do this based on the content of your discussion. If there's the slightest doubt about where to go next, ask for the order.

Consider the downside of this strategy. The worst thing that can happen is that the prospect says no, giving you a perfectly natural reason to ask "Why?" and find other objections or obstacles that might be lying in wait.

The bane of every salesperson's existence is the hidden objection—that obstacle to making the purchase that the prospect doesn't tell you about. It could be that the prospect doesn't like your proposal or needs approval for the decision from someone else. In any case, the hidden objection generally doesn't come out until it's forced out.

Another possibility is that your brilliant answer to the original objection wasn't accepted, but you don't find out until you try to close. In any case, your tactics will be the same: Use the four steps to handling an objection and start over.

There's no silver bullet for every objection. It takes a calm, controlled, persistent effort to listen attentively, restate carefully, agree amicably, and ask for the order over and over and over.

Remember, you're not there to bludgeon the prospect into submission. You want to use the proposal as a framework for finding a solution to the prospect's needs. You and the prospect are supposed to work together as a team and teamwork requires the give and take of information and ideas. This starts with an objection.

# CHAPTER 9

# THE THINGS
# THEY SAY

T he key to managing objections is the same as the key to a successful marriage—you've got to see things from the other person's point of view. You don't have to give in, just know where the other person's coming from.

In the last chapter, I covered the four steps in the Creative Selling System approach to managing objections. Let's go over some of the specific obstacles you'll likely run into in one form or another on every call. Some you can cut off at the pass—others you'll just have to grin and bear. In either case, it's important to understand what's going on in the prospect's mind.

You also have to have pretty thick skin and not let the slings and arrows get you down. Some people intentionally say downright mean and hurtful things when you're trying to sell them something. Fortunately, they are in the minority. A great many others, though not mean-spirited, will toss out comments like hand grenades, just to see how you deal with them—and just like a live hand grenade, you better deal with it right away.

You will face six common objections and obstacles:

## 1. I'M NOT INTERESTED

You've already anticipated this obstacle in the discussion about making cold calls. You may encounter it again, when you show up to make your presentation. But don't let it stand in your way. You've already overcome it once and you can do it again. Be encouraged—it's easier to manage this problem in person that it is over the phone.

Prospects who see you but then tell you they're not interested are contradicting themselves. They're playing poker—they're bluffing. All you have to do is call the bluffs without calling them liars. But first you have to determine whether they lost interest in your oral presentation, aren't interested in this specific proposal, or have no interest in your type of product or service.

## No Presentation Interest

If they're not interested in your presentation, you may not hear it in words, but you'll see it in their actions (or lack thereof) during your pitch. They sit and stare at you without changing expression. They look out the window. You really know you're in trouble when they start reading the newspaper on their desk

The best way to get the prospect interested is to ask a lot of questions. "Don't you think so?" "Doesn't that make sense to you?" "Does that match your experience?" These are all the kinds of questions you can throw in almost at will—and the more of them the better when you're in front of a poker face.

Don't get frustrated by one-word answers—prospects are trying to ruffle you by playing hard to get. Either way, you must keep control of the situation. If you respond to a one-word answer with an exasperated look, you've let them take control of your presentation. Be strong. Keep peppering them with questions and make them respond. This is a game of will.

## No Proposal Interest

If the disinterest is related to your proposal, do some probing. Make the subject of your questions the prospect's business and the way it relates to your proposal. Try to make your questions specific. "Does this investment fit in your existing budget?" "Have you ever done anything like this before?" "How do you think your employees will respond to this?" If you ask these kinds of questions you still may not make the sale but you will learn something about the prospect's needs that you can use in subsequent proposals.

As a last resort, you can always ask that nasty open-ended question, "Why?" Be polite about it and say something like "Your mind seems to be on something else. May I ask why?" or "You seem to have lost interest in our idea between the time I spoke to you on the phone and today. May I ask what's changed?"

But remember, "Why?" is a dangerous question. You have to be prepared for any answer. The good thing about "Why?" is that it doesn't allow for a yes-or-no reply. The bad thing is that you never know what you're going to get . Here are some of the responses to "Why aren't you interested?" that I've heard over the years:

❍ We tried that two years ago, and it cost us a lot of money. If I'd known that was your big mysterious idea, I'd never have agreed to meet with you in the first place.

## THE GREAT STONE FACE

I once knew a sales manager who had a deadly method of interviewing potential salespeople. He would shake their hands and invite them to sit down. And those were the last words he would utter. He would just sit there and stare at them impassively, waiting for them to start. The job candidate, of course, didn't know whether to talk or not. The tension would build to incredible heights, until the poor candidate either started babbling or ran from the room in a panic, which was a fairly common occurrence. This sales manager was sure he separated the wheat from the chaff that way. I think he was just indulging a streak of sadism.

But have you ever encountered a prospect that does the same thing? They just look at you? Don't run screaming from the room—have some fun! Pour on the enthusiasm with a bucket. Stand up and pace around the room while you're making your pitch. Wave your arms and jump around a little. It will be real hard for your prospect to keep on his poker face if he thinks he's in the room with a maniac. You're playing a role when you make a presentation, so act like you're Jack Nicholson in "One Flew Over the Cuckoo's Nest" if you have to.

The key here is enthusiasm. Remember, it's contagious—infect your prospect with it.

○ When you called I thought you said you were with TME, our biggest customer—not TNA, which I've never heard of.

○ My lawyer called just before you arrived to tell me we're being sued by the EPA.

○ My bookkeeper didn't show up for work today. I just found out he ran away with my wife after I left for work this morning.

I must admit these answers threw me at the time, but at least I learned something about the prospect in each one.

## No Interest In Your Product

The third variation on this theme are prospects who really contradict themselves by saying they're not interested in your type of product or service. If they weren't interested, why did they agree to the appointment? This is generally a smoke screen. All prospects are doing is making you earn your commission by putting on a good dog-and-pony show.

This problem is actually one of the easiest to deal with because you *know* it's a bluff.

Accept the challenge and put on a great show. Use the bluff as inspiration, and make the pitch of your life. Combine maniacal enthusiasm with persistent questioning and add one more element—blatant salesmanship.

Many prospects who use this ploy are in direct sales businesses or have a sales background. At the very least they admire a well-executed sales tactic when they see one. So give them what they want and use some of the less subtle techniques from the Creative Selling System.

Even if you don't make the sale, you'll establish yourself as a sales professional who isn't flustered by a little gamesmanship. That kind of reputation will get you in the door more easily the next time.

# 2. I DON'T NEED IT

Of course not. If the prospect knew he needed your product *he'd* have called *you*, right?

Don't let this nonsense get in the way of a good sale.

Actually, this isn't an objection. It's nothing more than a brush

## A RADIO DRAMA

I once tried to sell some radio advertising to a car dealer who opened our meeting by announcing "I don't listen to radio, especially your station. Nobody else does, either."

I tried some listenership statistics to prove he was wrong. His response was "Figures lie, and liars figure." I told him it wasn't important that he listen—just that his potential customers did. He countered with "If I don't listen, I don't expect they do, either." A brilliant mind at work, right?

Finally, I asked him how he knew nobody listened to our station. "That call-in show you have always has the same loudmouths calling every day. If you had more listeners, you'd get more callers," he said. If he didn't listen to the station, how did he know about the show? I took out a pad and began taking notes.

"That's interesting," I said. "Have you noticed anything else?"

"Well, now that you mention it, I don't know why you keep running that same commercial for Quick Eddy's Fast Food over and over again. Morning, noon, and night, all you hear is Quick Eddy's."

He got on a real roll then. "And I don't like that Gary Powers guy you have on in the afternoon. And that little girl who gives the news on Saturday always sounds like she's got a cold."

This went on for five minutes. The prospect demonstrated that his opening statement was nothing more than a shot aimed at provoking a response. By the time he finished his diatribe, he had sold himself a sponsorship of that call-in show.

You have to separate the real objections from the artificial ones.

off. It works pretty well, too, because there is no "answer" for it. You may have some cute comebacks, but they're going to backfire if you call the prospect a liar in one way or another.

You encounter this obstacle in several forms, often depending on the type of product or service you sell. People whose product benefit is an increase in revenues for the prospect (like advertising, for example) will hear "I've got more business than I can handle." Those who promise improved profits may be told "That just means more taxes." Another variation is the prospect who says "I'm perfectly happy with my present supplier." How can you argue with these statements?

You can't, of course—and prospects know that, which is why they throw them in front of you in the first place. So don't try to win the argument—just walk around it. When you encounter a statement like this, ignore it! Just say something to the effect of "That's interesting. Now, as I was saying. . ." and get back to your pitch. When you do, you'll probably discover that prospects forget all about this objection and consider your idea anyway.

This is a common smoke screen, so treat it as such every time. The worst thing that can happen is prospects bring it up again, signaling they meant it the first time.

This is true of every objection, of course, and it doesn't mean the end of the call. It just means you have to dig deeper into prospects' needs with some probing questions. If they don't need what you are proposing, what do they need? When you get the answer to that question, you're rounding third on your way to home.

# 3. I DON'T HAVE TIME

This objection usually signals a flaw in your proposal, or at least in your presentation. It might mean prospects like your idea but don't want to take on the task of executing it. It may also mean that prospects don't have time to *consider* your idea, which is just as bad, if not worse. Let's consider the first variation.

## Make It Easy

Business managers and owners are busy people. In Chapter 2, I talked about the many things they have to face every day—personnel, customers, taxes, inventory, and on and on. It's not unusual for a decision maker to like your idea but feel that he or she has too many other things to do every day to make it happen effectively.

In one way, that's a compliment to your presentation. You've probably built up the idea's value so much, it seems like more than it is. The prospect sees Buckingham Palace but you're selling a three-bedroom ranch on a quarter-acre lot. Examine your pitch and eliminate any exaggerations.

You should also examine the elements of execution in your idea. Are you asking prospects to do something to make the proposal work? Does their company have to provide additional training for its staff? Do they have to invest in another piece of equipment to use your product? If so, rework your proposal to include these items. Provide them yourself if possible. It may mean subcontracting a service or purchasing some equipment, but you're removing an obstacle to the sale. Charge your prospects for them (with markup), but don't make it their responsibility to make your idea work.

## Manufacture Time

The second variation, where prospects don't have time to consider your proposal, is a real problem. In this day of re-engineered and downsized corporations, more and more managers simply have too much to do. They are paid for their ability to make decisions, but they are given too many decisions to make. As a consequence, they limit the number of decisions by not considering new ideas. They embrace the status quo as a way of insuring they won't make a wrong decision.

> Above all, limit the number of choices and decisions prospects have to make to say yes.

Make the decision-making process as simple as possible. Promise that if they say yes to your idea, they won't have to deal with any of the details. You and your company will handle them.

Above all, limit the number of choices and decisions prospects have to make to say yes. A lot of proposals ask prospects to choose sizes, colors, dates, quantities, even models of equipment as part of the buying process. These choices have to be made, of course, but they should have been made before the presentation by the salesperson!

If you do your homework before the call, you eliminate the minor decisions. The worst thing that can happen is that you chose wrong. If that's the case, make the change on the spot and ask for the order.

Make your solution as turnkey as possible. This reinforces your position as an ally and resource. It's fine if the prospect wants to provide some of the elements, but don't make it mandatory. Since you built in a cost for all those elements when you structured the proposal, you may be able to use their exclusion as a negotiating tool.

Critically examine your idea for both of these problems.

# 4. I Don't Think It Will Work

This objection is a cry for help. Prospects like the benefits, but don't see how your idea can deliver them. You need to better explain the connection between the benefits and the idea.

Repeat and clarify—and above all, listen. What makes them think the idea won't work? Have they tried it before? Is there a flaw in your assumptions about their business? Any of these questions signal doubt in the idea's ability to deliver. Now is the time to probe and question—and listen carefully to the answers.

## Testimonials

There are several ways around this objection. One is to cite examples of other clients who successfully used a similar idea. Carry testimonials with you. (To get a testimonial, write it yourself then ask the testifiers to put it on their letterhead. Don't expect them to compose it.)

One caution about testimonials is that they have to be specific and verifiable to be believed. Too many salespeople have gone before you raving about "everybody" and "lots of people" using their products. If you want your testimonial to carry some weight, make it verifiable. Don't even think about making one up. Testimonials are like references on a resume. If one turns out to be a figment of your imagination, you're blacklisted.

## Demonstration

Another way to prove your idea works is a demonstration. Demonstrations were fairly easy when salespeople sold tangible products—you just brought along a sample (unless you were a loco-motive salesman). But what do you do if you sell services? You make them tangible.

I know a very successful TV ad salesperson who produced a videotape containing commercials from many of the campaigns she created. She uses it to show prospects the quality of her work. My friend Matt, the engineer-salesman, always carries a few copies of the detailed reports his firm prepared for his customers. In my con-sulting business, I sometimes offer a free short seminar for a prospect's sales force as a way to demonstrate the Creative Selling System. If you examine your service, you can find a way to make it tangible.

## When To Modify Your Proposal

There's another type of workability problem: when prospects just can't swallow some part of your proposal. For example, you may have proposed training programs for their clerks that take place after the store closes on Tuesday evenings. The prospect says that plan won't work because it generates overtime expense. If that's the only obstacle to the sale, go around it. Can you switch them to lunch time or provide the training in smaller groups during store hours? How about putting the training on tape and sending it home with them? There's always a way if you keep your mind open to the possibilities.

Unfortunately, the first inclination of many salespeople will be to say, "Let me work on that and I'll get back to you." That is about the worst thing you can do.

Prospect are saying they want to buy your idea but need help with an obstacle. Saying you'll get back to them is like telling a drowning person you'll be back as soon as you find a rope—they may not wait for you. Your prospects won't, either, or at least their enthusiasm will subside by the time you get back with a revised proposal.

Salespeople are particularly inclined to take this route when the obstacle is money. Let's put the reason into context. Remember, you're pitching a customer for the first time. As part of your prepa-ration, you estimated their potential spending and based the size of your proposal on that estimate. You fear you've built a skyscraper on a bed of sand.

When the prospect says, "I like your idea but I'm not sure I can afford it," you get a grip on your fear long enough to reply "What figure can you afford?" When you get a number, promise to come back the next week with a revised proposal for that amount. Then you rush out the door congratulating yourself on a sale made. The problem, of course, is that you haven't actually made the sale. All you've made is an appointment for next week. Lots of things can happen in one week.

So modify the proposal on the spot. You have a calculator, you know your product line and pricing, and you know the cost factors built into your proposal. You also have the prospect there to work with you on the revision, which gives you some great closing opportunities. Take a few minutes and revise the proposal right there. You'll immediately improve your closing ratio.

# 5. IT'S TOO EXPENSIVE

Ever heard that one? If you haven't, you've never made a sales call. I *like* to hear it because it means the prospect wants to buy my idea.

Remember the two questions the prospect needs to answer to make a decision:

1. What's it going to do for me?
2. How much does it cost?

Prospects only need to ask the second question if they like the answer to the first one. If your prospects don't like the idea, the price doesn't matter. Welcome the price objection with open arms. It means that the prospect likes your idea, and you have almost made the sale.

Understand why the prospect offers this objection. I don't know about you, but I make it a point to offer a price objection to every salesperson selling something I want. Your prospects do, too. The reason is simple: It gets them a lower price most of the time!

How do you manage this objection? The first step is to give it an automatic reply—ignore it. Acknowledge the statement and get on with your pitch. If the prospect brings it up again, answer it then. But the first time you hear it, pay no attention.

If you hear a price objection a second time, it's imperative that you listen to what the prospect is saying before you answer. Remember the video role-playing experience? Make sure you're answering the right objection.

There are several kinds of price objections, each requiring a slightly different strategy. Is the total investment beyond your prospects' means? Are the unit prices too high compared to your competitors? Or to your prospects' last order with your company? Does the price outweigh the value (benefits) of the idea? Know which one you're dealing with before you answer. The only way to know is to ask and listen.

## Can't Afford It

If prospects can't afford your idea, take something out so they can. Most of the time, they will say "I want the whole thing, just at a lower price." Good, now you know it's time to start negotiating. You've discovered that this wasn't a price objection, it was just the beginning of the negotiations. I'll talk about what to do next in this scenario in Chapter 11.

> Try to build the value of your idea rather than tear down the price.

But what if they *really* can't afford it? If you can't take out some value along with some dollars, come up with a cheaper idea. Keep in mind that the original proposal is based on your estimates, and they can be off target. If you're way off base and you can't come up with a cheaper idea on the spot, retreat and start over. Get as much information as you can about what the prospect can afford and what features he or she particularly liked. Then, set an appointment to come back with Plan B.

## Unit Price Objections

Objections to the unit price are negotiating tactics. Deal with them accordingly. Try to build the value of your idea rather than tear down the price. Review the benefits, expound on how the idea delivers them, and stress the unique nature of your idea.

Make sure you don't lower the price without taking away some of the value. Otherwise, you're just negotiating with the prospect, and this is not the time in the sales call to do that.

## MAKE YOUR OWN BED

**A**ny time you have a prospect doing price comparisons, take a cue from the mattress business. Do you know how mattress retailers can make the offer "If you find the same model elsewhere for less, we'll give you the mattress free?"

It's because the mattress manufacturers put a different model name on each retailer's line—they're the same product in every store, just with different labels. So the customer can never find the exact "same model elsewhere"!

The mattress industry got in some serious trouble with the Federal Trade Commission about this tactic, but you can do this honestly if you practice true creative selling.

If you're selling an idea developed expressly for each of your prospects, they really can't get it elsewhere. That means they can't make apples to apples price comparisons. That's one of the biggest advantages of the Creative Selling System.

# Price Increases

If customers have done business with your company before, they probably have a pretty good idea of what they paid for the last order. If they're any kind of good businessperson, they'll check the last invoice, just to make sure. If your prices went up, watch out!

When customers object to a price increase, most salespeople immediately defend and rationalize their pricing. Their first instinct is to tell customers they're just passing along the increased cost of doing business. The cost of raw materials has gone up or the last union contract carried a big wage increase for their company. All this may be true, but quite frankly, customers don't care. Those are your company's problems, not theirs.

Instead of defending your price increases, why not brag about them? We live in a supply-and-demand economy. One of the responses to increased demand is higher prices. If increased demand is the justification for your price increase, you're really saying that more and more customers are recognizing the value you offer. That reinforces your prospect's decision to buy. This rationale will only hold up as long as it's based on truth. Don't claim rising sales if they don't exist.

A much better strategy is to avoid rationalization and justification in the first place by practicing sound creative selling. If you've presented a new idea to customers, they can't compare its price with the last order any more than they can compare it to your competitors'. This is particularly true if you follow the Creative Selling System written proposal strategy and don't present unit prices in the first place. Remember, ideas are unique—and so are their prices.

## The Price/Value Equation

The majority of price objections are buying tactics and should be dealt with accordingly. One that's generally not a ploy, though, is when prospects say that the value of your proposal is less than its price. If that's truly their perception, you need to take a completely different tack.

Now is the time to make sure you're telling prospects about the benefits of your idea, not the features of your product. Benefits have value, features have price tags.

This is also the time to repeat your benefits and get prospect agreement on each one. It's likely that prospects forgot or overlooked some of your idea's benefits during the presentation.

You can also bring out any "minor" benefits which you haven't covered yet. They may not be insignificant to prospects, so load them on if you need to. The only way to tilt the price/value equation in your favor is to increase the perceived value.

# 6. I DON'T LIKE YOU

Let me tell you a short story. I was selling radio advertising at the time this happened. One of my accounts was the branch location of a national mobile home sales company. I had a good rapport with the manager of the lot, who spent a significant amount of money. The sales cycle was straightforward: I saw him around the middle of each month to set up the schedule of spots for the next month.

One day I walked into his office to make my usual pitch. As usual, my client Jerry was sitting behind his desk, but there was another man, who I didn't know, talking on the phone in the next office. Since Jerry invited me in, I sat down and began my spiel. When I got to the proposal, which was always for about twice as much as I actually expected to get from Jerry, he started shifting in his seat. His face was bright red by the time I asked for the order. When I asked my closing question, he jumped out of his seat and started shouting!

"I'm not spending this kind of money with you! What's wrong with you? What kind of pigeon do you think I am?"

Needless to say, I was startled. But I kept my cool and tried to get the pitch back on track.

"Gee, Jerry, we can always work up a smaller package. What do you want to spend next month?"

## GET A SECOND OPINION

It's usually a good idea to get a second opinion before you undergo major surgery. The same holds true for giving up an account due to a personality clash.

Most of us aren't very accurate when it comes to judging our own popularity. Those of us with low self-confidence think nobody could possibly like us while those with giant egos are sure that everybody does. This problem doesn't get any easier with customers, many of whom are playing hard-to-deal-with as part of their buying procedure.

That's why it's a good idea to ask for a second opinion before you give up an account. The first and best source for that opinion is probably your sales manager. Second would be a senior salesperson or an experienced colleague. Ask them to call on the account with you, but only to observe, not to present. Their experience and knowledge of human nature helps them pick up personality conflicts

Sales managers can also call on the customer or even make a telephone inquiry. If they're discreet, the customer will never know they're investigating a problem. And you'll get the second opinion you need before you authorize that amputation.

"I'm not spending a dime with you!" His face was so red, I thought he was going to burst a vessel. "Get out of here!"

And with that, Jerry doubled up his fist, leaned across his desk and took a roundhouse swing at me!

Fortunately, I ducked. I also beat a quick retreat without even offering "This must be a bad time. I'll get back to you later." Jerry had just handed me an objection I didn't know how to handle. Self-defense was not covered in any of my sales training.

> The root of the problem may be anything or nothing, but you can't attack it until you know what it is.

This is a rather extreme example, but sometimes there is an obstacle that has nothing to do with your idea or your presentation. It is a strong negative feeling that prospects have about your company, your product, your boss, or even you. It can have a rational basis or be entirely emotional. It can be a cold shoulder or a wild punch. It says "I don't like you, so I'm not going to buy anything you have to sell."

If you've never run across this problem before, keep making calls and you will. It happens to everybody.

There are two strategies for dealing with this problem. One is to give up and move on. If the problem is bad chemistry between you and the decision maker, this is the best route to take. If a prospect hates redheads and your nickname is "Carrot Top," don't fight it. You have to weigh the economics, of course, but you can't change your nature and you certainly can't change anyone else's.

If it's not just a personality conflict, take another route first before you giving up the account. Try to get to the bottom of the problem. Don't argue with prospects who say "Your company stinks." Ask why they feel that way. Was it a bad past experience? Poor service from the last salesperson? Mistakes in the last order? Did your company's president back into the prospect's car in the country club parking lot? The root of the problem may be anything or nothing, but you can't attack it until you know what it is.

Once you know, do what my boss told me to do with Jerry—apologize. Even if you're right and he's wrong, *you* apologize. Even if he swung at you first, you apologize. The customer is always right, and apologies make sales.

My boss made me go back and see Jerry the next day. I wanted police protection, but my boss assured me it wouldn't be necessary. Jerry was cold when I got there, but at least he wasn't swinging at me. Even though I felt very strange about it, I gave him my apology.

"I'm sorry my proposal or something wasn't right yesterday," I said. "To make it up to you, we're going to give you some free spots on your schedule this week. Is that OK?"

Jerry then apologized to *me*.

"You don't have to do that. I shouldn't have done what I did. That was my regional manager in the other room while you were here and he'd just chewed me out for going over my advertising budget. You came in right after that. Sorry."

Jerry reacted to my apology out of guilt. He knew he was wrong, but didn't want to admit it. My apology gave him a graceful way out. He could not only say he was sorry but make amends by turning down the free spot. If I hadn't apologized, he probably would have fumed for weeks, if not forever.

The offer of some free product may seem uncalled for, especially in this case. But even if Jerry had accepted it, it would have been a small price to pay compared to the loss of his business. Even though these can be emotionally charged situations, you have to base your strategy on long-term economics. What do you have to do to get past the obstacle?

Have I handled all the objections? Good, let's go to the next chapter and close the sale.

# CHAPTER 10

# ALWAYS LEAVE
# THEM SMILING

losing the sale is the most misunderstood selling skill. It's probably also the most overrated. Regardless, there's no question that closing causes the most sales-related antacid consumption.

It doesn't have to be that way. There is no mystery behind closing. It's not a hard skill to learn or to practice. If you are concerned about it, just keep in mind that the goal of every sales call is simply to leave behind a happy customer behind.

## CLOSING
## MYTHOLOGY

The big misconception about closing is that predatory salespeople set traps for unsuspecting prey with clever ruses and mental manipulation. This view assumes prospects are dolts, easily tricked by clever closing techniques. Nothing could be further from the truth.

Most of my prospects—and I'm sure most of yours—are pretty smart people. They wouldn't be in decision-making positions if they weren't. They are good buyers who consider all the pros and cons before making a decision. They negotiate hard until they get a deal they can live with. They certainly aren't naïve.

## Short- And Long-Term Relationships

A familiar sales adage says you should close early and close often. That's a clever way of defining the salesperson's job as getting the order at all costs. The problem with concentrating on closing skills is that it shifts the emphasis away from developing long-term customer relationships. One mark of managers or owners with this attitude is how much they boast about their team's high closing ratio.

These people believe that actions that form long-term relationships—researching the prospect, making multiple proposals and revisions, focusing on meeting customer needs—consume too much time. They divert the salesperson's attention from the real job at hand, which is generating orders. "Let the long-term relationships take care of themselves," they say. "I've got to make this month's quota." To them, long-term customer relationships are fine, but what really matters is the order brought in the door today. And if enough orders are written each day, long-term relationships don't matter.

> You should approach closing with the idea that every sales call gives the customer another reason to do business with you.

That's true as far as it goes. Where that shortsighted philosophy doesn't go is into the realm of profit margins. The long-term customer is almost always the most profitable one as well.

This short-term philosophy is also the exact opposite of the Creative Selling System, where one of the major goals is the creation of long-term customer relationships. You should approach closing with the idea that every sales call gives the customer another reason to do business with you. It's a proactive, pro-customer way to look at your job.

## Complex Sales

Closing is vastly overrated. If you practice the Creative Selling System, you rarely get a chance to close because clients buy before you ask for the order. That's how the approach is designed. About half of all successful sales calls end this way. You don't close the sale—it just happens.

This is particularly true for products and services where several complex decisions are involved. A complex sale doesn't occur in one sales call—or even two or three. It may take weeks or months of presentations and revisions before prospects give you the order.

In complex sales, a classic closing opportunity may never arise. Instead, your relationship with the prospect evolves into a partnership with your proposal at the center of it. What "closes" that sale isn't any clever technique but rather the tenacious effort you put into the proposal.

The salesperson who pushes too hard to close a complex sale often blows the opportunity altogether. It's one thing to be aggressive. It's quite another to back the prospect into a corner. Don't send the message that you are more interested in making today's sale than becoming a long-term ally.

# CLOSING MADE SIMPLE

If half your sales close themselves, that means that the other half won't—and half don't feed the bulldog, or even the poodle. It's this *other* half of the time that closing skills come in handy.

These situations are a lot like marriage proposals: Some prospects won't say yes until you ask them to. Maybe they're reluctant to make the first move. Maybe they're waiting for a better offer. There could be a whole host of reasons, but regardless of why, it's time to ask for the order

Many salespeople get nervous about closing because they make too much out of it. They overwhelm themselves trying to figure out which set of magic words to use. Salespeople also create their own anxiety because they *know* they're not going to fool the prospect. They know prospects aren't stupid. They fear the prospect will catch them in an artificial maneuver and resent them for it. Or, even worse, laugh at them for trying it.

Don't fret about it. All you have to do is ask a simple question: "Do you want to buy this now?"

There are numerous books about overcoming the fear of closing—most of them based on the incorrect premise that salespeople fear rejection. Salespeople deal with too much rejection to fear it. What they fear is looking foolish.

## THE HEAD-NODDING CLOSE

**A** great number of salespeople practice what I have come to call the head-nodding close. In this particular maneuver, the salesperson won't ask a closing question verbally, but when a natural closing opportunity arises (like naming the price of the proposal), the salesperson vigorously nods his head up and down.

I've considered many explanations for this behavior and have finally concluded that salespeople who practice this move are hoping the prospect will start nodding along with them.

Besides looking rather silly, the head-nodding close doesn't work very well and, in my book, it doesn't count as asking for the order.

Let's add another goal to the Creative Selling System. Let's not only leave the prospect smiling, but make sure you're smiling, too.

I learned a lot about sales behavior when I started videotaping role-played sales calls. So did my training clients. One of the most interesting things I learned was how many times a salesperson thought they had asked a closing question when, in fact, they had not. They wouldn't believe me until they saw themselves on tape during the playback and critique.

# TIMING THE CLOSE

Before I talk about *how* to ask for the order, let's consider *when* to ask the question. In some ways, the timing of the close is more important than the words you choose. You may have the most compelling, romantic marriage proposal since Napoleon wooed Josephine, but if you deliver it at the wrong time, you're likely to stay single longer than you hoped. Timing is everything.

Ask for the order when you see any one of several buying signals. These are actions prospects takes that tell you they might be ready to say yes. These actions are sort of like the "tells" that a professional poker player watches for. When you observe a buying signal, it's time to pop the question.

One buying signal is when the prospect is paying extra close attention to something you're saying. They may have nodded through the first five minutes of your presentation, grunting non-committally when asked a question. If they suddenly sit up straight and their eyes come alive, take it as a buying signal.

Another signal is voluntary agreement with your points. I'm referring here to a prospect who says "Yes, I agree with that" without being asked. That's voluntary agreement. This happens when prospects are so wrapped up in the presentation and so enamored with the idea, they forget they're being sold. This buying signal often precedes a sale that "just happens" without a closing question. Don't count on it, though, and remember you have nothing to lose by asking a closing question at this point.

"How" questions are very strong buying signals. They generally mean that prospects have moved beyond the "should we" phase of consideration to the "how do we" phase. They're offering you the opportunity to remove the "can't" obstacle so they can give you the go-ahead. This is a good sign because "can't" comes after "won't" in the logical sequence of a buyer's decision-making.

The lights are flashing green, mission control is completing the countdown, all systems are go. What do you do now?

## The Closing Question

Go with the flow. If it's appropriate, review the point that sparked the buying signal and ask for the order. "I can tell you appreciate this high impact widget. Would you like to order a dozen now?" This type of closing question will either give you a yes or prompt the prospect into telling you what he really wants. Either way, you've come out ahead in the exchange of information.

But what if this is one of those prospects who won't be rushed? What if this is a complex sale that's not going to happen on this call? Are you harming future chances by closing too hard? Only if you're trying to close without first receiving a buying signal. If that's the case, you'll have plenty of opportunities to change direction and recover lost ground if you practice the first rule of creative selling—listen!

When you ask for the order, shut up and listen. I've said it before and I'll say it again: You make more sales with your ears than your mouth. The most important part of the close is not the clever way you phrase the question, it's the amount of attention you give to the answer. Good closers aren't fast talkers, they're fast listeners, ready at all times to hear what the prospect has to say.

Ultimately, you'll find that closing is more of a process than an event. It'll often occur over several calls, not just within the context of one presentation. As a rule of thumb, the larger a proposal (in dollars or length of commitment), the longer the prospect will take to make a final decision. Again, if you're practicing the Creative Selling System correctly, you're focusing your efforts on large proposals to large accounts. You should not expect to close every sale on the first call.

What you should try to do, however, is mark some progress on each successive call. Think of your relationship with the prospect as a journey you're making together. Sometimes you travel through known territory at a fast clip; other times you slow down because the road is slippery. Sometimes the two of you will make detours to avoid major obstacles. Along the way, you'll mark your progress toward an ultimate destination—the point where the prospect agrees to exchange money for your goods and services. Try to make some measurable progress on every call.

## Persistence

Never give up! Don't let your enthusiasm wane after three or four calls without an order. It may seem like the prospect is wasting

### A Trial Offer

**M**uch has been written about trial closing, which is a technique where you ask a closing question early in the pitch without any real expectation of getting an order at that point. I like this technique because it prompts the prospect to talk, which is never a bad idea.

If you look closely at the format for the Creative Selling System presentation, what you're really doing is a series of trial closes when you ask a question at the end of every page. You're asking the prospect to buy the benefits, then the idea, and finally the proposal.

Every one of these trial closes generates feedback that tells you which direction to take next. But you'll receive that feedback only when you listen for it.

your time. But keep in mind that the single most effective closing technique is to keep trying. Keep learning about the prospect's needs and pitching more ideas. That's the way to close a sale. Remember that not every journey ends at the original destination.

# CLOSING TECHNIQUES

Now let's talk about techniques that make closing the sale a positive experience for both you and your prospects. Every salesperson has a favorite close. I've covered some in other chapters, but now let's spend a little time detailing some of the most common ones.

I have two goals here: to help you find a standard closing that works for you and to give you an arsenal of alternatives to try if your standard close isn't appropriate. Think of the various closing techniques as encores to the original close since you seldom get an order the first time you ask for it. As I discussed earlier, you may have to revise your proposal on the spot to deal with an objection. This means you'll need to ask for the order again.

I'm also going to cover the most common obstacle you face: the prospect who won't say yes or no, but always gives you a "let me think about it" answer.

## The Direct Question Close

My favorite closing technique is also the simplest: the direct question. I also think prospects appreciate this type of close because it's the most honest. It doesn't sneak up on them. It treats them like mature, responsible businesspeople, able to reach quick, firm decisions.

My favorite direct question is, "Would you like to make this investment today?" Since I'm usually selling a fairly expensive consulting service proposal that pays off in the long run, the term "investment" suits the offering very well.

I also use the imperative "today" because I'm trying to get a commitment from the prospect now—not later. That word serves as a signal to them that it's yes-or-no time. If you want to use the direct question method, find words of your own that fit your product or service line.

## CLOSE ONCE MORE...WITH FEELING

I once led a sales team working to get a contract with a potentially lucrative prospect who heard our pitch several times over a period of nearly two years, but wouldn't give us a yes or a no.

We had to do something. We sent gifts, tried president-to-president meetings, pitched revolutionary mixes of services, but nothing provoked a definitive response.

Finally, in an internal review, someone remarked that the decision makers were all football fans of the major university located in their town. A little research indicated that most of them would be in the stadium on game day.

I hired a skywriter to fly over the stadium, streaming the message "Prospect Company belongs with Our Company." The plane circled the stadium for an hour and the decision makers couldn't very well avoid it.

Monday morning, a call came in from the decision maker. He said that we had made a great impression on them and they were ready to switch their account as soon as their current contract expired. That was the good news. The bad news was that their contract had just automatically extended for another two years.

Before that time expired, I left that company to start my consulting business. This prospect became one of my first clients, mainly because of our persistent presentation of attention-getting ideas. The act of closing never got in the way of making the ultimate sale. I kept them smiling throughout the process.

Some other direct questions you might try are:
○ Would you like to do business today?
○ Can I order this for you now?
○ Do you want this plan?
○ Are we in agreement on the deal?

The direct question needs to be short and sweet. It should not have any "wiggle room" for the prospect to use to back out of the commitment. It should be strictly a yes-or-no proposition. If prospects want to say maybe to a yes-or-no question, they have to work at it.

It's important to use your own words for the direct question close. They have to be natural. If you seldom use magniloquent words in normal conversation, don't stick any into your closing question. If you're a distinguished-looking professional man or woman, stay away from an MTV vocabulary, dude.

Write down your closing question (and a few variations) and read them aloud. You'll be able to tell pretty quickly if those words belong in your mouth.

## The Benefit Review Close

The direct question is my favorite closing technique, but I certainly recognize and use others that may be equally effective. In fact, another closing technique, the benefit review, is basically the one I use in the Creative Selling System presentation. Recall that once you've named the price of your proposed idea, you turn the page, review the prime benefit, and ask for the order.

This technique is grounded in the fact that your prospect buys the benefits you're offering, not the product or service you're selling. That's why the benefit review strikes closest to the heart of the buying decision.

Another reason I like the benefit review method is because it encourages prospects to talk about their needs and wants. If you're not getting anywhere reviewing the prime benefit, go over the others as well, pausing after each one to ask the prospect how he or she feels about it. Each time you get a particularly positive response, ask for the order.

If you get a negative or neutral answer, don't try to counter it or argue; probe for more information. Either way, you'll move the closing process along.

## The Minor Decision Close

Closely related to the benefit review is the minor decision close. The difference is that you ask the prospect to make an intermediate decision about the product or service before making the final decision to buy your proposal.

## DANGER WORDS

There are a few words and phrases I generally avoid. One is "commitment." People don't make commitments lightly—they think about them, review them, sleep on them before they make them. Commitments are final. Commitments last a long, long time.

Another touchy phrase is "sign up" as in "Can I sign you up for this program?" People sign contracts, but only after they've read them thoroughly and had them studied by their lawyers. Whenever you get a lawyer involved in a decision, it will take three times as long and be six times as complicated.

Even if prospects don't consult a lawyer, they'll wonder if they should, which gives them another reason to delay making a decision. If you need a signed document, ask prospects to OK the order on the dotted line.

No matter how you phrase your closing question, make sure to use only positive action words. "Do you think you might like to maybe make this investment someday?" doesn't carry the same persuasive force of "Would you like to make this investment today?"

Take a look at your list of closing phrases. Did you use "might" or "maybe" anywhere?

Strike those two words from your vocabulary along with "I think" as in, "I think this is the best plan for you." That says this is only your opinion— and you are admitting that the prospect could have a different opinion.

These are fine points, but the little things add up to the prospect's total impression of you and your offerings. You want the prospect to see you as someone with total confidence in your products and yourself.

When done properly, the string of minor decisions takes away the obstacles one by one until there is no real reason not to make the final one. It also builds a positive team attitude as you and the prospect shape the proposal to best suit each others' needs.

When using the minor decision method, try to project an attitude of "*If* you were to buy my proposal, would you prefer option

A or B?" so prospects don't feel any obligation in making an intermediate decision. When you do this, it makes the minor decision method a good one to use on prospects who seem to have a hard time making up their minds out of fear of making the wrong big move. Making the minor decisions with your help gives them confidence to make the final decision.

On the other hand, you don't want to use the minor decision close on a prospect who can't seem to make a decision! People like this fear both large and small decisions. They are especially hesitant to make quick decisions, so your request for a series of intermediate decisions could slow the sale. You'll encounter enough of that problem without causing it yourself.

The minor decision close allows you to test the waters before you plunge into the big question. If you're getting a lot of resistance to the little things, you don't want to shut down the opportunity by pressing for a final decision. You may want to probe their thinking a little to see if there are any obstacles lurking under the surface. It's easier to do this before you ask for the order than afterward.

## The Deal Maker Close

Another closing technique is one that requires equal amounts of finesse and brute strength. It's the deal maker close. The deal maker is essentially a quick, hard negotiation. It's particularly effective when used after an objection or when struggling to modify a proposal to fit the prospect's needs. The exchange goes something like this:

The prospect says "I'm not sure I like this feature of your proposal."

So you reply "If I take it out, can I have your order today?"

It's put-up or shut-up time for the prospect. Done correctly, it's not as dangerous as it might seem for the salesperson. If the answer is yes, you obviously have the order. If the answer is no, you have a natural opening to ask why and learn more about the prospect's needs. You also find out if there are other objections.

The two dangers in the deal maker close lie in the words that are used and the authority the salesperson has to modify the proposal. If the salesperson doesn't phrase the offer correctly, the prospect can say yes without placing an order. This happens when the salesperson says something like "If I make the change, will you *consider* the deal?" The prospect can easily agree to consider the deal without buying it, so the salesperson hasn't advanced the sale.

The second problem with the deal maker close is when the salesperson makes a deal without authority to do so. More times than not, the price of the proposal is involved. If the salesperson can't adjust prices on his or her own authority, the deal maker close based on pricing should not be used. What are you going to do if you shook hands on a deal only to have it rejected by your sales manager when you get back to the office?

> **If you can make adjustments in your proposal and you have the brass to make a "put up or shut up" offer, the deal maker close is highly effective.**

Some salespeople will try to work around this problem by making an offer contingent on approval by a higher authority. I don't care for this since it reeks of the old used car salesman's "Let me see if I can sell this deal to the big boss" routine. Everybody knows the salesperson just goes into the back room with the "big boss" to smoke a cigarette and tell a couple of jokes. Either way, the prospect is left wondering if the salesperson can be trusted—and that's no way to start a relationship with a new customer.

But if you can make adjustments in your proposal and you have the brass to make a "put up or shut up" offer, the deal maker close is highly effective.

## The Alternatives Close

In this technique, you let prospects choose between two courses of action, either one of which means they have agreed to buy. You don't list "no sale" as one of the options, of course.

The alternatives close is the ultimate assumed close. It assumes prospects have already decided to buy, even though the words have not been uttered, so all they have to do is confirm it by making a choice.

This method is popular because it is actually a little charade both the salesperson and the prospect can play, avoiding that sometimes ugly, tension-filled moment when the salesperson asks a direct question and the prospect has to give a direct answer.

I find this method a little too manipulative and denigrating to the prospect. It's as if you're saying "I don't think you're smart enough to see through this." I base this opinion on my own reaction when someone tries to use the alternatives close on me.

The biggest problem with the alternatives close is that it opens the door to delays and the delayed decision is the salesperson's most dangerous enemy. The problem is, once you've laid the alternatives out on the table, you have no place to go if the prospect says "Gee, I don't know which one I prefer. Let me sleep on it." After all, you brought up the options. Now are you going to make them rush the decision?

# GETTING BEYOND DELAYS

Why do prospects make you wait for a decision? There are several reasons, most of them legitimate. Some prospects are afraid of making a decision, especially on the spot. Others really want some time to consider your proposal. They are deliberate in their approach to decision-making.

I've encountered customers who won't buy anything over $1,000 until they've slept on it. Maybe they want more information from another source. Maybe there's another decision maker or influencer involved. Or maybe they just want to give themselves some time to reverse their line of thought.

Most of the time, prospects who say "maybe" are just too nice to say no. They don't want to hurt your feelings or they're afraid you'll launch into another song and dance about the benefits of your proposal. They know they can get rid of you by telling you to call back next week. And you not only accept that response, you embrace it with open arms because you're too nice to pressure them into a hasty decision.

Most salespeople welcome "maybe" because it's not "no." "Maybe" releases the tension that's been building in the salesperson since the beginning of the call. That tension mounts as you build your pitch to a climax of asking for the order.

Nobody likes tension. Accepting "maybe" is an easy way to remove the tension and get away from its source—the prospect.

The first step in overcoming delays is to stop deluding yourself. "Maybe" isn't even remotely close to "yes." "Maybe" is just a polite

## THE SADDEST COUNTRY SONG

The delayed decision causes so many heartaches and headaches I'm surprised Garth Brooks hasn't written a song about it. If you've made more than one sales call in your life, you've heard a prospect say "I'll think about it." That's when the sad saga begins.

You call back at the appointed time, usually about a week later. You say "Have you reached a decision?" and they reply "Sorry, not yet. Try next week."

Next week rolls around and they're out sick on the day of the appointed call. The next day they say "Sorry, I was sick and couldn't think about anything. Give me a few more days."

The next time you call, they don't return your call for a couple of days. And on and on and on.

Most likely, your proposal went onto the pile of other proposals, bills, letters, and junk mail, where it was covered up by the proposal of the salesperson who had the appointment following yours. Within 10 minutes of leaving the prospect's office, your proposal has received all the consideration and attention it's ever going to get.

Don't get caught up in this delusion. When prospects insist on "I'll think about it" even after you've tried my delay-busting tactics, assume the answer is no. Make the follow-up appointment anyway, but come back at the appointed time with a new idea. If they were really thinking about your original proposal, they can always say so. If not, you've saved several weeks in the selling cycle by creating a new opportunity.

way to say no—and "no" is an acceptable answer! Getting a "no" means you can move onto another idea.

Don't give in to the tension-relieving impulse and automatically accept "maybe." Do yourself and the prospect a favor and press for a yes-or-no answer.

You can probably think of some others, but here are three closing methods to try when faced with a delay.

## The Ben Franklin Close

The first is the Ben Franklin close. The prospect says she wants to think about the proposal and you say "That's a good idea. Let's draw up some points for you to consider." Then you take a blank sheet of paper and draw a line down the middle.

At the top of one column you write "Reasons No" and the other "Reasons Yes." Then you proceed to fill out the page, beginning by asking the prospect to list all the reasons she shouldn't buy your idea. Then you list all the reasons she should.

At each point, of course, you have the opportunity to either overcome an objection or to ask for the order again, or both. And that's the purpose of the exercise. If the prospect can list more "Reasons No" than you can list "Reasons Yes," you deserve to lose the sale. But at least you've eliminated that week's delay while she pretends to "think about it."

## The Columbo Close

Another delay-killer is the Columbo close. In this scene, you play Peter Falk's role of the disheveled TV detective who always seemed to have one more point to make that he "remembers" as he's leaving the suspect's office.

As you're on your way out the office door, proposal neatly packed in your briefcase, turn and say "I just remembered an important point for you to consider while you're thinking about the proposal this week. Can I have just another moment of your time?"

The idea is that you will catch the prospect with his guard down. When you headed for the door, he felt as relieved as you were that the pressure to make a decision has been put off for a while. So when you launch into your pitch again, his defenses are down and you can go for broke. Now make just one more salient point and follow it up with a good, hard closing question. Just like Columbo catching the bad guy on TV.

## The High-Noon Close

The last method to overcome delay is the High-Noon close. This time, instead of playing the part of a TV detective, you're Gary Cooper in the movie "High Noon," gun on your hip and ready for the big showdown. This is the close of last resort because you're going to tell prospects that you're not going to accept maybe. They have to tell you yes or no.

"I can appreciate your needing some time to think about my proposal. Unfortunately, I need an answer today. If your decision is no that's fine—I'll see you next week with another idea. If it's yes we can start work on this right away. So what's your answer, yes or no?"

Be polite, be gracious, but be firm—just like Gary Cooper. There comes a time in every person's life when you have to take a stand.

You'll find that very few prospects resent this close. They generally see it for what it is, a timesaver for both of you, and respond accordingly. If they were going to tell you no later, they'll say it now. If they are truly going to think about it and there's a chance they might buy, they'll tell you that also. Once again, you come out ahead in either scenario.

I'm sure you'll find a closing technique that fits your personality and style in this sampling. Try each one out and see how they feel. For each method, ask yourself whether you are comfortable using it. Does it fit your personal style? Will the one you choose leave the customer smiling? Remember, that's the purpose of the close—to create a happy customer.

# CHAPTER 11

# NEGOTIATE TO WIN?

**D**o customers in your industry pay the asking price or do they routinely ask for a lower price, better terms, extra merchandise, rebates, slotting fees, or extended service? If you sell business-to-business, you've probably never had a customer agree to pay your asking price on the first pass. What your customers are doing, of course, is practicing an art as old as commerce itself. They're negotiating.

Negotiation is that stage of the selling process that occurs after the commitment to buy is made but before the sale is actually closed. It's when the buyer and seller come to terms on the conditions under which the product or service is provided.

Sounds imposing, doesn't it? And it can be a complicated undertaking, which is why I suggest you approach negotiations as carefully as Beethoven approached composing a symphony. You need to coordinate all the various components of the negotiation if you are going to produce a successfully orchestrated sale.

## NEGOTIATION CHARACTERISTICS

Negotiation is a matter of choices by both parties. One party chooses whether to offer something and the other one chooses whether to accept it. As you'll see, it's not always the seller who does the offering, nor is it always the buyer who does the accepting or rejecting. Nor is price the only item subject to negotiation.

When do you negotiate? If you're a creative seller, you only negotiate the terms of your proposal after the prospect has made the commitment to buy the idea you are selling. As I said before, if the prospect doesn't like the idea, no amount of negotiation will make the sale happen. But once that commitment is made, you will negotiate every sale in one way or another.

The price-to-value ratio is at the heart of every negotiation. Both the buyer and the seller negotiate both sides of that equation. When the needs of both the buyer and seller are met, the sale occurs.

## Firm Prices

Some people are leery of negotiating a sale. They feel that the process is somehow dishonest or demeans them, their product, or even their prospect in some way. In fact, I often encounter sales managers who proudly point out that their prices are firm. They insist that every customer pays the same price and that's the one set by the sales manager or owner. They would rather forgo a sale than violate their holy pricing policies. These people need a strong dose of reality—and they often get it in the form of declining market share.

> If you're a creative seller, you only negotiate the terms of your proposal after the prospect has made the commitment to buy the idea you are selling.

There is nothing holy about a given price, nor is there any moral law that says that every customer is entitled to the same terms. In fact, I think you could make a pretty strong case for customizing prices and other terms according to each customer's needs. If you want to carry the moral argument to its logical end, how do you justify denying a customer the benefits of the product or service you are selling solely on the basis of the price they are able or willing to pay? You don't want to go down that road.

Don't get me wrong. There's nothing wrong with having a firm pricing policy. But let's not hide the reasons for it in some kind of moral cloud. Firm pricing is a matter of what management feels is best for the selling company. Ideally (from their standpoint), it controls demand to produce the maximum profit from the available supply. And having firm prices makes the administration of the revenue stream easier, which makes the sales manager's or owner's job easier. There's nothing wrong with that.

But there is nothing wrong with negotiating every sale, either. Humans have been doing it for thousands of years. In fact, the most successful economic system yet invented, the free market economy, is predicated on the freedom of sellers to offer different value for various prices and for buyers to accept or reject them.

In business-to-business sales, nearly every sale is negotiated. There may be published price lists and standard terms, but very few buyers would keep their jobs if they didn't at least try to do better. And few sellers would keep the revenue flowing if they didn't make pricing adjustments to stay competitive.

# WIN-LOSE NEGOTIATION

So how do you negotiate honorably and successfully? By negotiating both value and price with the goal of striking the most favorable deal for *both* the buyer and the seller. If there is a morality problem with a negotiated sale, it's when one party's aim is to win the game at the expense of the other. If both the buyer and the seller can believe in and practice win-win negotiations, everybody's life is easier and they can sleep better at night.

Unfortunately, too many people engage in win-lose negotiations. They believe that the only way they can gain value is by taking it away from the other person. They view every transaction as a zero-sum game. This belief is against the Creative Selling System. You can't build long-term relationships with customers you take advantage of. Sooner or later they figure it out.

When you engage in win-lose negotiations, you create an adversarial relationship with your prospect. That lifeblood of creative selling, information about the prospect's needs, is cut off at the source because the prospect soon realizes that you're using that information to gain the upper hand in the negotiations.

That's one of the main reasons the traditional consultive selling approach is so ineffective—many prospects fear that giving information to the consultive seller will just give him ammunition to use in future negotiations. So they clam up or give out misleading information.

You can't create solutions to the prospect's needs unless you learn what those needs are. Without that information, your selling effort degenerates into a guessing game where you have to keep offering different proposals without having the necessary feedback to come up with good ones. When your ideas don't meet the prospect's needs, fewer sales occur. The win-lose negotiation attitude may produce a larger single order today, but it reduces the probability of getting better orders tomorrow.

# Win-Lose Disadvantages

Win-lose negotiation also produces conflict, which drastically reduces the efficiency of the buying and selling process. Both parties waste valuable time plotting negotiation strategies, floating trial offers, and delaying commitment until they are reasonably sure that the other side has given up as much ground as they are going to. "Never leave money on the table" becomes the goal of the seller rather than "Create a satisfied customer."

Win-lose negotiation focuses almost exclusively on price, with a resulting denigration of value. Buyers may get "more for their money" but that's just a perception they have because the seller lowered the price. In the world of win-lose negotiation, buyers are only deluding themselves thinking the seller hadn't jacked up the asking price in the first place.

They may actually get less value than if they paid a slightly higher price. That's because sellers who are caught in win-lose negotiation often react by lowering the value delivered. Production and shipping priorities tend to favor the customer who pays a higher price. After-sale service does the same. Special offers aren't offered to the win-lose buyer because the seller knows they'll try to knock the price down even further. Consequently, that buyer may miss some real values at bargain prices.

And buyers who "lose" in win-lose negotiation retaliate, too. If they feel they've been pressured into a corner on the price, they'll remember and get even next time. They'll look for another supplier. They'll pay the invoice at the last possible moment. They won't think twice about canceling an order at the last moment.

The only time you should engage in win-lose negotiation is when you aren't concerned about repeat business. That's why some negotiated transactions have a reputation for being ruthless. Real estate, business ownership sales, and other onetime transactions are often conducted on a win-lose basis because the two parties generally have no economic connection or even contact after the sale closes.

## Negotiation And Stress

Negotiating has earned its reputation as an unpleasant process in large part because it is inherently stressful. Each party creates stress by blocking the other's goals. "I won't buy unless you give me this" is just another way of saying "You can't obtain your goal (to get the order) because my demand (to get the concession) is blocking your way."

Two other stressful things happen in negotiation. The blocks generally get bigger after the easy concessions are made early, leaving the tough ones—the big price cut or the large volume order—to the end. The closer you get to the end, the closer you are to achieving a goal.

The uncertainty of the outcome is stressful. The pressure to make multiple decisions is stressful. The fear of feeling outfoxed is very stressful. It's certainly a lot easier to say "Sorry, our prices are firm. Take it or leave it."

# WIN-WIN NEGOTIATION

Negotiation doesn't have to be that way. I'm not saying that you'll eliminate the uncertainty, the decision-making, or the possibility of leaving some money on the table, but you can make the process less stressful if you have the right attitude.

The better way, of course, is win-win negotiation, where both parties recognize that the value side of the equation is not finite. If you can focus on building the value of the deal, both the buyer and the seller generally win. Win-win negotiation is at the heart of the Creative Selling System because it focuses on need satisfaction.

It's an attitude thing. Win-win negotiators may start from completely polar positions, but they're going to meet somewhere in the middle, not drag each other from one side to the other.

This type of mutual conflict resolution builds trust, which opens the doors to better communication of needs. Creative sellers practice win-win negotiations to get the information they must have to meet prospects' needs.

The lack of conflict builds efficiency into the buying/selling process. I remember once trying to negotiate a TV advertising schedule with an advertising agency that practiced win-lose negotiation. If they had approached the situation with a win-win attitude, we could have struck a deal within minutes. But because they were intent on squeezing the dollar until Washington screamed, the negotiations went on for two weeks. They still didn't get a better deal, but they wasted a huge amount of their time (and mine).

## Value, Not Price

Generally, the focus of win-win negotiations is on value, not price. The seller has a tendency to add more value to the package rather than cut the price and the buyer has a similar tendency to ask for more value rather than to demand a lower price. Both parties are more likely to meet in the middle because they are not giving up money.

The final solution better meets the needs of both parties. The seller gets a larger sale in terms of dollars and the buyer gets a better solution to their need in terms of value. Most important, a foundation is laid for a constructive future relationship.

"Only in the land of milk and honey," say the skeptics. "It's a tough old world out there."

Skeptics are right about some things, of course. It is a tough old world. But I've found that the people in that tough old world are pretty nice—if you're nice to them first.

Somebody has to make the first move. The next time someone asks you for a lower price, try offering more value instead, then wait to see how they react. If they're intent on pounding down your price, you'll find out soon enough. But you'll be surprised at how often people will respond positively, opening the door to a trusting relationship.

## GOT VALUE?

**W**hat are some value items you can offer to help close a sale? They vary depending on the product or service you sell, but keep in mind that "value" doesn't have to mean "free stuff." Value comes in many forms:

**Terms of the Sale**
- ○ Payment due dates
- ○ Size of credit lines
- ○ Carrying charges
- ○ Discounts for prompt payment
- ○ Length of grace periods

**Related Items**
- ○ Product exclusivity
- ○ Advertising support
- ○ Trade promotion

**Future Sales**
- ○ Price guarantees
- ○ Contract extensions
- ○ Cancellation privileges
- ○ Volume rebates

**Product/Service Features**
- ○ Delivery dates
- ○ Production line priority
- ○ Special packaging
- ○ Service guarantees
- ○ Warranty extensions

**Miscellaneous**
- ○ Quick decisions
- ○ Referrals
- ○ Contract length
- ○ Volume of order
- ○ Share of business

Some of these items are price-related, but most are not. All, however, represent a form of value to either or both parties.

This is certainly not an exhaustive list—I'm sure you can develop a list of your own that relates to the product or service you sell. Even two or three items that carry little cost to the provider and high value to the receiver can be good negotiating tools.

# INFORMATION IS POWER

In all types of negotiation, information is power. Win-win negotiation is no exception. In fact, the more information both parties have, the smoother and more productive the negotiation can be. The things you want to know are much the same as those you want to know about your prospect when you develop your proposed idea for them.

Remember they will want to know the same kinds of things about you and your position, so be prepared to offer some of that information under the right circumstances. Conventional wisdom says that you should play your cards close to the vest, but sometimes the exchange of information can be a transaction within a transaction that smoothes the larger negotiation.

## Sources Of Information

You have many sources of information at your disposal. The prospect is the best one, of course, and if you've been listening to him as well as talking to him, you'll have already picked up the answers to many of these questions. Don't overlook your company's files, either. A prospect may be new to you but not to your company. The salesperson who preceded you in the territory may have had some contact with the prospect.

I've also found it useful to get to know my customers' employees. You certainly want to know their secretaries or assistants as well as the receptionists and switchboard operators. But don't overlook the salespeople, clerks, shipping manager, buyers, purchasing manager, bookkeeper, etc. You never know when they're going to reveal an interesting tidbit of information that you'll find useful during negotiation.

The prospect's competitors and other vendors are important sources of information, too. A caution in this area, though: You don't want to become known as a rumormonger. Such a reputation has far-reaching consequences. Keep your ears open and your mouth closed.

Always consider the source when judging the truthfulness of any information. A little knowledge can be a dangerous thing, especially when it's exaggerated by a partially-informed employee or a competitor with its own agenda. Just as information can be helpful in negotiation, misinformation can be disastrous. Anyone who has used stock market "tips" can attest to that.

Honesty in negotiation is important in another sense. Be honest with yourself about your own position. You tend to underestimate your own strengths and weaknesses because you are more aware of them than you are of the buyer's. Remember, the buyer probably doesn't know that you're just one sale away from winning that trip

## BE A KNOW-IT-ALL

Here's a partial list of common types of information you should have before you enter negotiations:

○ What are the prospect's apparent needs?

○ Do any underlying needs exist?

○ What are the alternatives to your proposal?

○ What are the advantages/disadvantages of the alternatives?

○ How do your competitors fit into the alternatives?

○ What is the prospect's financial position?

○ How big a factor is the price?

○ How strongly are they committed to the proposed idea?

○ Are there other decision-influencers?

○ What deadlines are they facing?

○ Are they negotiating win-win or win-lose?

to the Bahamas. If you reveal that fact, you'll probably pay for it by suffering through a more demanding negotiation.

# NEGOTIATING TACTICS

Everybody has their favorite "rules" for negotiating. But rules can be dangerous if you don't temper them with common sense. I've learned the hard way that you can outsmart yourself if you try to get too fancy in your negotiating maneuvers. Let's look at some common tactics.

## Time Pressure

One of the factors never to be overlooked in any negotiation is time. Time pressure works for and against both parties, often in interesting ways. Anyone who has been involved in union negotiations, for example, knows that the largest concessions always come just before the strike deadline. In fact, sometimes that's the first time *any* concessions occur. Knowledge of the other party's deadlines is a powerful tool.

The pressure to come to an agreement is generally greatest on the party with the nearest deadline. Magazines are more inclined to negotiate liberal terms for ad space the day before the issue closes than they are the week before. The prospect whose insurance policy is about to lapse is more eager to renew the policy than one with a 90-day grace period. Know your prospect and know their deadlines.

One way to use time to your advantage is by making small concessions, drawing out the negotiating process. On the other hand, you may need to bring the deal to a close, in which case you may want to make a BFO, or best-and-final offer.

As a seller, don't be surprised if the buyer calls your bluff. They have nothing to lose and plenty to gain by telling you your BFO isn't good enough. If you back down and make a further concession, all you've done is prove to the buyer that you're a bluffer.

The time to make a BFO is when you discover you're negotiating with yourself. You can tell because the other party isn't offering any concessions—you're the only one making any movement. It's one of the most frustrating situations you can face. You make all the moves, getting nothing more than "That's not good enough" in return. The time to take a chance and make your BFO is when you have nothing to lose.

## Starting High

I used to be a strong advocate of aiming high—making an outrageous offer so that I'd have plenty of room to come down when the buyer made a counteroffer. Besides, I believed low offers signal weakness.

I eventually learned that if the first offer was *too* high—outside the realm of what's reasonable to the buyer—then the buyer might not make any counter-offer at all. Then where was I? If I lowered my offer to restart the negotiation, I was really signaling my desperation and letting the buyer know that concessions could be won.

Carefully judge the plausibility of your opening offer. Now my rule is that my opening offer is one at the high end of what the prospect could accept—and one I could defend without stretching my credibility.

## DO YOUR HOMEWORK

Remember the first step in the Creative Selling System? It's gathering information about your prospect. And one of the key pieces of information is an estimate of the prospect's spending potential.

This not only gives you a goal to shoot for and an idea of how to structure your proposal, but it gives you a good guideline for where to start your negotiations. As long as you begin with a proposal in the ballpark prospects are used to playing in, you're not likely to scare them off.

Take the time to do your homework, and use one or more of the estimating methods I covered earlier. Even if you didn't use those figures to structure your proposal, they will give you a sense of the possibilities for your negotiation.

## Lowest Acceptable Alternative

I've also acquired a little discipline. At the beginning of the negotiation, I like to establish (in my own mind) the lowest acceptable offer I'll take. That way, I have a sense of how far I can go before I start cutting into profit margins, production capacity or whatever benchmark I'm using. As the negotiations proceed, I know where I am at all times and that sense of security gives me greater confidence.

Establishing the lowest acceptable alternative in advance does something else. It keeps me in a win-win frame of mind because I don't have to worry about losing. As long as I know the point at which I will walk away (and stick to it), I can't lose anything.

As you may have noticed, I've now set an upper and a lower limit to my pricing. This range makes it much easier to build a few small concessions into my proposal or plan some value items I can add as the negotiations proceed. This helps me avoid making that big concession all at once, leaving me with no place to go if the buyer rejects it.

## Never Give Without Getting

One rule I've found very helpful is to never give a concession without getting something in return—or at least asking for something back. If you don't, you'll end up negotiating with yourself. Only in this situation, the buyer keeps the process going by making more and more demands. You can control this too by asking for something in return. For example: "If I extend your warranty, will you buy the extra large assortment?" It's a not-so-subtle reminder that negotiation is a two-way street. It's also a graceful way to avoid saying no.

Rarely use "no" in negotiations of any kind. It's so final, so definite, so negative, that it should only come into play when you've been pushed to the edge of the cliff and the buyer demands you jump off. To avoid being pushed that far, try saying "maybe."

## The Power Of Maybe

If you are negotiating in win-win mode, "maybe" keeps the door open to add value items until the entire deal is clearly structured. When two people sit down at the negotiating table, they each usually have a list of items they must have, ones they'd like to have, and ones that they'll take if offered. One form the negotiation can take is for both parties to exchange lists, then discuss each item.

For this format to work properly, of course, there must be total honesty and complete trust on the part of both parties because you have to be sure there are no items held back. Because of this requirement, this type of negotiation seldom occurs in its purest form. The temptation to have a few cards up the sleeve is too great.

You're never sure if the demand for a sweetener will pop up the end, so you don't say yes or no to any single item until all items are on the table. You say maybe to each one until you are pretty sure you have seen all the items the other person wants.

Then you give a conditional "yes" to a package of values that you are comfortable giving. The condition of the offer is, "If you buy this exactly as offered, I'll give it to you at the agreed price." If the prospect agrees to this deal and then tries to get more in the package, you're able to honestly say that you have to revise the price.

Saying maybe works the same way when you don't have the buyer's want list at the beginning. A common negotiating strategy for buyers is giving just enough information to get a proposal out of the seller. When you're faced with that situation, saying maybe is the only way to get more information. If you say yes or no to each item as it comes up, you're handing complete control over to the buyer.

# Structuring The Proposal For Negotiation

The seller's want list is usually contained in the proposal as offered. As I mentioned before, it's a good idea to build some possible concessions into your proposals. The number and type will be determined (at least in part) by whether this is a new prospect or a repeat customer. You won't know the negotiating habits of the first-timer but you probably have some knowledge of how a repeat customer behaves.

You may also want to hold back some value items as a sweetener. These can be optional features you throw in at little or no cost such as extended payment terms.

There are a couple of cautions to this practice. For one thing, if you consistently hold back and then give the same item to a customer, they will consider that item a standard part of future deals and it will lose its value as a sweetener. You also have to be sure that your sweetener isn't offered until the end of the negotiation. If you even hint at its existence earlier, you will lose its impact in your closing.

When you're faced with negotiations to close a sale, look on them not as a hassle but rather as an opportunity to close. Always keep the ultimate goal in mind: You're negotiating to make the sale, not to win at the buyer's expense.

# CHAPTER 12

# PLOT TWISTS AND TURNS

T he sales I've described up to this point have been pretty simple. You find the prospect, research their needs and develop an idea, pitch the decision maker, manage the objections, close the sale, and negotiate the order. Straightforward, isn't it? Nice and linear.

But selling in the real world isn't quite that simple. The "normal" sale is about as linear as a nest of worms. You may be able to find something that looks like a beginning, but which of the squirming bodies is at the other end? Welcome to the world of the complex sale.

The complex sale is easy to identify but hard to complete. You'll know you are in the middle of one when the prospect says "I really like this idea, but I have to run it by my boss." And then his boss says "Good idea. What does production have to say about it?" And then production says "Interesting. Can we change these widgets into wodgets—if the new assembly line we're installing next year calls for it? Better check with the vendor." So the vendor of the new assembly line says "We'll set it up any way they want. Besides, what's a widget?" Get the picture?

There is a decision maker, but there are also multiple decision influencers. There is ultimately a yes-or-no decision, but there are also multiple interim decisions to be made before that point is reached. It's a recipe for mass confusion.

Successfully completing a complex sale requires tremendous patience and perseverance, two qualities often in short supply among salespeople, who got into sales because they like the instant gratification of closing a deal. If the reason you get up and go to work each morning is to see how many sales you can make in a day, I suggest you find something simple to sell (like Girl Scout cookies) and a simple market to sell it in (like sole proprietorships with fewer than two employees). Selling just about anything else to larger organizations requires the ability to navigate through a complex sale.

I'm going to look at the individual components of the sales process and discuss techniques for dealing with each one. When I finish, you will have a map to follow to reach the end of the complex sale labyrinth. Let's start with the people involved.

# DECISION INFLUENCERS

Have you ever heard this sales adage: Never take no from someone who can't say yes? There's more than a kernel of wisdom in it, but this truism undoubtedly predates virtual corporations with horizontal organization charts describing the functions of an empowered work force. In most complex selling situations, you're going to find that the first hurdle to overcome isn't no, it's identifying all the various players with something to say about the decision.

When it comes to identifying the people involved in a buying decision, I often refer to decision influencers rather than decision makers. That's because there are many people in the modern business structure who don't have the authority to say yes or no but whose opinions are solicited by the decision makers. Even seemingly simple decisions often go through the influencer mill. This happens for a variety of reasons.

For one, a large number of today's executives practice consensual management. The old autocratic "buck stops here" decision maker is out of sync with the latest in management theory. These modern executives believe (and rightly so) that involving more people in a decision improves their acceptance of that decision.

There's also a widespread belief that the more people involved in a decision, the better that decision will be. It's a safety procedure often practiced by decision-makers who prefer to spread the risk among a larger group.

And then there's the modern management buzzword, "empower-

## IT'S NOT THE SIZE THAT MATTERS

The dollar size of the buying decision doesn't necessarily dictate the number of decision influencers involved. One of the more interesting sales I ever made was a multimillion-dollar communications tower to a company in Saudi Arabia. The situation had all the hallmarks of a complex sale.

The purchasing company was a joint venture operated by two other companies, one French and one Saudi. The item I was selling was a very high priced component in a much larger complete system, to be operated by a ministry of the Saudi government. The construction manager was an Egyptian subcontractor to the Saudi/French joint venture.

Even the payment wasn't linear. Their funds came from an insurance settlement still in dispute. The payment was to be made in the form of an Irrevocable Letter of Credit, which had to be approved by the Saudi bank, our bank, and a transmitting bank in Switzerland.

Despite having all the potential for generating an endless chain of meetings, referrals, studies and opinions, the sale was closed after a single 90-minute meeting with the president of the joint venture and the construction manager.

On the other hand, I also sold a small-market TV advertising package worth $300 that required four weeks of study and deliberation by an advertising agency's media planner, buyer and account supervisor; their client's store manager, regional manager, and advertising director; and the co-operative advertising manager of one of the store's vendors. The FedEx and long-distance telephone bills were greater than our profit on that sale. The moral of the story? Watch out, a complex sale could be lurking anywhere.

ment," which supposedly pushes decision-making further down the chain of command. Companies who empower their employees will proudly tell you that you don't have to pitch your product to The Boss because any number of subordinates can make the final decision. The Boss will go along with anything they decide. To me, just saying that she will go along implies that she also has the option to *not* go along.

Unfortunately, at least in my experience, many of the employees who have been empowered don't want the responsibility that goes along with the territory. They feel threatened by the responsibility that comes with decision-making. They may even feel that upper management is copping out on their responsibilities by pushing decisions down in the organization. They're much more inclined to say no than yes because keeping the status quo is a safer decision. They also push the decision back up the corporate ladder—or worse, don't make any decision at all.

The biggest reason you'll constantly be involved in complex sales is that the fabric and structure of many industries have become more complex. The mom and pop grocery store has given way to the megamart. The independent local realtor is now a franchisee of a national financial conglomerate. Waves of consolidation have swept through every industry from radio broadcasting to funeral homes.

And with size almost always comes complexity. The management of a nationwide group of cable systems has a vastly more complicated structure than the one running your local antenna service. There are system managers reporting to regional managers reporting to division managers who draw on the resources of the corporate marketing, finance, legal, engineering and administrative staffs. The decision to buy a new digital switcher, for example, may have to be approved by a dozen individuals. At the sole-proprietor cable TV service, one person—the owner/operator—makes that decision.

Since creative sellers focus on large accounts, they pursue the national organizations rather than the mom and pops. You must develop a set of tools and tactics to reach and persuade the multiple decision influencers in your prospect's company.

# THE DECISION PROCESS

As you work on complex accounts, you must learn to be patient because you're in for a long ride. Multiple decisions made by multiple decision influencers means multiple calls, meetings and proposals. Sometimes you'll be fortunate enough to get everyone involved in a decision into one room at the same time—but that will be the very rare exception rather than the rule. For the most part, you have to count on individual pitches delivered over a period of weeks or even months.

And, because there are so many cooks involved in flavoring the broth, you'll have to count on making numerous modifications to your proposal. Just about every time you make a change, you have to take the newly modified proposal back to the people you've already pitched. It seems like an endless process, but getting that big order is worth it.

> As you work on complex accounts, you must learn to be patient because you're in for a long ride.

One of your first steps is to identify all the decision influencers, which can be difficult. Figuring out who among them are the most influential is even harder.

Keep careful notes of each meeting. Weeks after the call, you won't remember each individual's input. Determine who reports to whom and include that with your data.

## Gatekeepers And Flak-Catchers

Many times you'll have to fight your way through an army of flak-catchers to get your proposal in front of the people who matter. Flak-catchers are those people author and social commentator Tom Wolfe identified as the ones sitting in the outer office whose job it is to intercept incoming shrapnel, complaints and sales pitches to protect the real decision makers inside.

There's a great temptation to try to blow right by the flak-catchers and get to The Boss. The problem with this tactic is that it backfires too often. You never know the dynamics of their relationship. Many busy executives take cues from an administrative assistant because they work so closely together. Assistants know just how much power they have, too, and won't hesitate to use it if they feel slighted. Remember how much trouble Marie Antoinette got into because she brushed off the concerns of the little people.

You also have to be careful about job titles. Does the Senior Vice President of Marketing make the final advertising budget decisions? Does the Operations Manager buy the production line equipment— or does that job belong to the Purchasing Manager? Maybe. Maybe not. It all depends on the company and practices. You obviously need to do your homework and ask lots of questions as you're working your way through the maze.

## Problem Decision Influencers

The decision influencer that will really drive you crazy is the invisible one. I don't know how many times I've worked for months on a prospect, making endless presentations to person after person only to get a final no because I missed an unidentified decision influencer along the way. You can't count on the prospect to offer guidance, so remember to ask for it.

> Cover all your bases, and make the presentation to anybody you can corner long enough to hear it.

Another source of sales insanity is the self-appointed expert. Every prospect seems to have someone on staff whose responsibility is to pass negative judgment on every sales proposal. They're always hardest on the proposals that didn't start in their office—an interesting coincidence.

Some products and service lines draw these experts more than others. More than half American homes have computers, so you can count on at least half the prospect's employees having an opinion on your product if you sell information systems. And everybody is an expert on advertising, of course, since we're exposed to it every day.

## Overriding Strategy

The strategy I've adopted to deal with all these contingencies is to make the presentation to anybody who will listen to it, whether I think they're directly involved in the decision or not. With a complex sale, you can never be sure who's doing what or who has the stroke, so cover them all. Since a complex sale can take time (weeks, months, or even years) to complete, the person you've pitched may get promoted, transferred or terminated before the final decision is made. Cover all your bases, and make the presentation to anybody you can corner long enough to hear it.

That goes for various associated procurement services, too. Advertising agencies, merchandise buying cooperatives and consulting firms heavily influence prospects' buying decisions. In fact, they often perform much of the "heavy lifting" when it comes to routine buying decisions, taking the mundane administrative burden off the shoulders of the actual buyer. They earn their keep in savings for the prospect.

You cannot go around these people—they'll get you in the end if you do. You must also make sure your proposal doesn't stop on their desk. If you follow the guidelines in this chapter, you can be sure your idea gets beyond these dead ends.

## Complexity Of Your Product

Another complex element of today's selling process is the sale of services and product systems rather than items. You don't sell a line of widgets; you sell "widget-based interior manufacturing process solutions." You don't sell a bookkeeping service; you sell "digital financial management decision and accounting information systems."

The more complicated the product, the more "experts" required to make a decision about buying it.

## Major Roadblocks

One of the many pitfalls in a complex sale is the "whisper down the lane" problem. You've probably played that parlor game where one person whispers a phrase to the next person, who repeats it in the ear of another person until "Mary is going down to see Phil" becomes "Mary's gong rang on Sea Hill."

This is going to happen to you and your proposal when a flak-catcher says to you "The Boss is too busy to see you now, but I'll explain your proposal to her for you." This is not a good thing.

Not only are flak-catchers unlikely to get your proposal right, it's a given that they won't deliver it with the same enthusiasm and positive energy as you would. In fact, they're likely to start the pitch of your idea with "I don't know if you'll like this, but. . ." and go downhill from there. Remember, it's their job to say no to proposals, so they have to at least imply that answer to The Boss.

That's if your proposal makes it into the inner sanctum at all, of course. Most of the time, you get that routine for the same reason a prospect says "I'll think about it" rather than giving you a simple no. It's a convenient, low-risk way to get rid of you for a while. In fact, when you call back to see how The Boss liked the idea, the flak-catcher can tell you "no sale" and blame it on The Boss. You have no way of knowing whether The Boss actually saw it or not.

This same problem is magnified when you're forced to deal with buying agents. They have a vested interest in keeping The Boss in the dark about your proposals and will go to great lengths to make sure you don't even think about going around them.

# THE COMPLEX SALES CAMPAIGN

When you're faced with this problem, approach it carefully but aggressively, following the steps I recommend *in their exact order*. If you jump ahead, you'll suffer the consequences.

*Step One:* First, establish contact with The Boss. Contact doesn't have to mean a face-to-face meeting. In fact, at this stage you don't really want a face to face. Put The Boss on your company's direct mailing list. Make sure she gets your newsletter, press releases, and new product announcements addressed to her personally, with a brief FYI note signed by you.

*Step Two:* When you present a proposal to flak-catchers or buying agencies, follow it up with a thank-you letter and carbon for The Boss. Make sure the letter praises the flak-catcher for perception and professionalism during your meeting. Do the same if you get an order. Lay it on real thick. It'll make them look good to The Boss—and how can they object to that? That letter, of course, will also put your name in front of The Boss, establishing a contact with your company.

These steps can't be rushed. Together, they'll probably take at least four to six weeks. You have to judge the time you need according to each situation, but remember that the relationship must evolve over weeks, not days.

*Step Three:* After you lay the foundation, build the relationship. This step will probably require at least another four weeks. Get some face-to-face contact with The Boss. Invite her and the flak-catcher to one of your company functions. If you don't have any events where customers are welcome, think about staging one. Throw a cocktail party to announce a new product or a buffet lunch in appreciation of past business.

If your company gives away any goodies—coffee mugs, T-shirts,

## ROUND AND ROUND

Here's a scary number: 27. That's the number of yes-or-no interim decisions that need to be made in a committee where just three people decide whether to buy an item with three specifications. Each person has to consider and agree with each of the others on each possible combination of specified features.

What's really scary about that number is that it does not include the final yes-or-no buying decision!

Eliminate as many of the interim decisions as possible when you put together your Creative Selling System proposal. If you give the committee just one decision to make (buy or don't buy), you've eliminated all of the interim decisions.

---

caps with your logo—be sure to give one to the flak-catcher *and* one to The Boss. Hand-deliver them if possible. Your goal is to put your face with that name The Boss has been seeing on correspondence for the last eight weeks. If you have to leave The Boss' gift at the front desk, put a hand-written note with it.

Get your management involved. If you are a manager, get a colleague involved. If your boss or associate invites The Boss to dinner, the flak-catcher can't take it out on you, especially if the dinner is a social affair. Most top management recognize the importance of these occasions and consider them part of the job.

*Step Four:* After you establish a pattern of contact with The Boss, pitch an idea to her.

Send a letter to The Boss much like your cold call telephone appointment pitch—promise her an idea and ask for 15 minutes of her time. Send a copy of the letter to the flak-catcher. Then call the flak-catcher and ask if he is available for the meeting. Don't ask permission—assume the close and invite the flak-catcher to the meeting. Finally, call The Boss and set a date and time.

The worst thing that can happen is that the flak-catcher gets irritated by your end run. But what can the flak-catcher do? Tell The Boss that she shouldn't meet with that nice person who sent her all those gifts, invited her to dinner, and sent her that wonderful letter praising the flak-catcher's performance? It's hard to do that without sounding petty and defensive.

Is the flak-catcher going to tell you not to call The Boss? It's possible, but if you invite him to the meeting too, he'll have a tough time justifying the demand.

*Step Four Alternative:* What if The Boss still won't take your call? There's always Plan Two, which is your fallback strategy when you can't get in to see someone. I'm sure you remember this—put your pitch on videotape and send it to the prospect. The only difference here is that you send a copy to the flak-catcher or buying agency as well.

Videotaping a presentation is a good way to avoid "whisper down the line" problems and the difficulty of making multiple presentations to multiple decision influencers. This is particularly true if they are spread over the globe, as is often the case. It may not be as much fun, but it's a lot more efficient to send a videotape to the regional manager in San Francisco than to fly out for a meeting.

## To Your Battlestations

What do you do when the buying agency forbids you to contact The Boss?

Don't go into that battle without reinforcements. Be prepared with a thorough analysis of the buying agency's past purchases from you for The Boss' company and any others it may represent. What's the worst-case scenario? How much current business could you lose if the buying agency carries out its threat of no longer doing business with your company? How much future business? Some tough decisions will be made, and you need as much information as you can gather to make them.

If you decide to enter the battle, go all out. This is no time to be tentative. Reinforce your relationship with other customers who do business through the buying agency by calling on them. Visit The Boss and ask him directly if he wants to be denied your ideas. Then go see the buying agency management and see if they're willing to soften their position.

If they won't relent, cut them out of the loop and deal directly with The Boss. You need to be strong when you're battling the forces of evil.

# Ideas, Ideas, Ideas

Regardless of how you deliver the presentation to The Boss, it's paramount that you present an idea, not a list of product features. Bosses hire flak-catchers and buying agencies because they don't have time to make routine decisions. They're usually the "big picture" people who get paid the big bucks because they make the big decisions—so give them a big idea to make a big decision about.

As long as you are an idea seller, The Boss will see you—even if she doesn't buy your first idea. She'll admit you to the inner sanctum if you have the price of admission—an idea she can use. But she'll relegate you to the lobby with the rest of the peddlers if all you have to sell is a bag of product.

An idea is the engine that drives the sale through the many layers of a complex sale. If you are selling an idea, all the decision influencers are interested in hearing about it. If your idea is strong enough, it won't be changed by everyone in the decision-making hierarchy. Ideas sell, especially in the face of complexity.

# CHAPTER 13

## LOOKING FOR ADVENTURE

**I**t may seem a little backward, but now that I've used thousands of words to describe how to make a sales call, it's time to talk about how to choose who to call on. Actually, it's not as backward as you might think since knowing what you do when you get there will help you choose where to go in the first place.

I'm going to talk about prospecting—that process in which you gather and screen a list of potential customers to find those you can most *productively* sell.

Many salespeople hate the very thought of prospecting. It smacks of cold-calling, door-to-door canvassing, and rude telephone calls during dinner time. Besides, it requires a lot of work that often does not result in a sale. They prefer "qualified" leads: ones that have requested a salesperson's call. And many companies have systems to do just that. But company-supplied leads shouldn't preclude your own prospecting.

The most successful salespeople I know grow their income by assiduously adding new accounts. They prospect constantly. They don't dread the cold call; they thrive on it. They love the challenge of meeting new people, learning about different prospects, and making revenue appear where none existed. They have a nose for the hunt.

Regardless of which category you fall into, there's a strong likelihood you'll need to do some prospecting at some time. Let's talk about some of the methods you can use to make the process as pain-less and as productive as possible.

# COLD CANVASSING

Cold canvassing is the first method that comes to mind when most people think of prospecting. You go door-to-door or make phone call after phone call until you find someone who might be interested in buying your product. In cold canvassing, you make a standard intro-ductory presentation to prospects and get them to respond with information that determines whether they are likely customers.

This is also known as the "mud against the wall" style of selling. If you throw enough mud, some sticks. If you call enough people, some are bound to need your product. Except for salespeople with certain masochistic tendencies, this method is generally not one with a lot of fans.

It takes a lot of effort and time to make cold calls, and it's about as creative as digging a ditch. The only way to make it work is to keep doing the same thing over and over. But guess what? The ditch gets dug and your muscles get stronger. This method would have died out years ago if it didn't produce sales.

Cold canvassing has its place in the Creative Selling System, but you have to make some compromises. First, while you do need an idea to present on your first call, you probably can't have one for every prospect. Create a generic idea that best reflects the benefits your company has to offer. If you don't have an idea to present, you waste a lot of time and energy just handing out business cards.

Second, you can't have a custom written presentation for each prospect. Use a generic version of the five-page proposal form and print a stack of them to use on your calls.

Your goal on the cold canvass call is the same as on your first call on any prospect: Get information. Since you have an idea to present on the cold canvass call, get responses to it that you can use on sub-sequent presentations.

## Canvassing Fun

Set aside one day a month for cold canvassing. Take the generic proposal I just described and pitch it to as many different businesses as you can in one day. Set some specific goals, like making a pitch to every business on the south side of Main Street between First and 10th Avenues. Call every business in the Yellow Pages from "banks" to "bed and breakfasts."

I've found that a good time to spend the day cold canvassing is when I'm feeling a little down. A day of cold calls is a great cure for the "blahs." If nothing else, it blows out your mental cobwebs.

Don't get too picky about who to call on, either. This is like brainstorming—quantity, not quality, is what counts. The only administrative task I suggest is that you keep a list of everybody you call on, noting anything you learned on the call. Put a star next to the prospects who deserve a follow-up call with a custom presentation in the Creative Selling System format.

> Above all, have fun. Look on this as an adventure full of unknown people and unexpected events.

Above all, have fun. Look on this as an adventure full of unknown people and unexpected events. Don't worry about making a sale. Try out some new "reasons to buy" or a package of services you've wanted to test. See if that unsold inventory in the back of the warehouse will move at break-even prices. Make it different and make it fun.

Cold canvassing can be a lot more interesting if you do it with other salespeople. You can make a contest out of it. The person who makes the most calls, or the most sales, or turns up the most prospects is the winner. Meet at a coffeeshop a couple of times during the day to compare notes and war stories. It'll make the day go faster and the break will help keep your enthusiasm up.

## Category Canvassing

Another prospecting method which is more consistent with the Creative Selling System is category canvassing. This technique is often used by salespeople whose products or services are sold to a variety of businesses. For example, if you sell office supplies, or insurance or advertising, you may have clients ranging from grocery stores to swimming pool contractors. When you use the category development technique, choose one type of business and pitch them all the same thing.

You need to do a little homework when you use this method, following the prescribed routine of researching the prospects' needs, estimating the potential, and preparing an idea-based proposal. This sounds like a lot of work if you're pitching 15 different funeral homes in your territory.

It's actually a time-saving technique because your research will reveal the same needs for each of the 15 prospects. The first idea you come up with is the same one you will pitch to each of the prospects. All you do is change the name on your presentation. Pitch that idea until someone buys it. The odds are great that you will never get to the last name on the list because someone will buy the idea first.

## Benefits Of Category Canvassing

One of the advantages of this method is that you'll learn something more about the category on every call, allowing you to make each successive presentation more effective. It's a lot like calling on the same prospect once a week for 15 weeks, only in this case you're calling on 15 prospects once. You add to your store of knowledge with each meeting.

I recommend you start with the smallest prospects. Why? You want to hone your presentation before you get to the biggest prospects. Practice and make your mistakes on the small accounts so you have a better chance of closing the largest ones.

If you work with a group of other salespeople, there's a great temptation to divide the category among yourselves. This is a more efficient way to cover the category, but it doesn't help the learning process because it cuts down on the number of prospects each salesperson is exposed to. If you decide to work as a team, make sure you get together at the end of each day to compare notes.

# REFERRALS

One of the very best ways to pick up good prospects is by referral. You usually think of getting referrals from current satisfied customers, but don't limit yourself to that group. One of my good friends and competitors in the consulting field asks every person he pitches for a referral to someone who might be interested in his

## ONE HAND WASHES THE OTHER

I've done business with the same insurance agency for many years. In fact, since the agency is a family affair, I have watched the children grow up and take over the business from their father. From time to time, one will call me with the name of a potential prospect. And I do the same for them.

When my wife and I sold our home, our realtor brought a couple relocating to our area to see the house. Afterward, the realtor told me that the prospective home buyer saw some of my sales literature on my desk at home and asked him what my company did.

The couple ended up not buying our house, but I followed up on the lead (which turned into a short consulting project) and gave my new client the name of my insurance agent since I figured he might need one, being new in town.

My insurance agent got the business. I'll have a chance to return the realtor's favor one of these days, too.

services. If the original prospect doesn't buy, at least my friend gets something of value for his time.

The best part of getting leads by referral is that you get to draw on the source's body of knowledge about the referral, as well as your own. Most of the time, they give you insights you wouldn't necessarily find on your own. They may also identify a new prospect you hadn't considered.

Most people are happy to do you this favor as long as it doesn't carry a high cost to them. Never use their name when following up on the referral without explicit approval in advance. Your source doesn't need to write a letter of recommendation. All you ask for is the name of the person you should see. If your source offers to call them or write a letter to introduce you, all the better, but don't push it. If you can get a name, you have enough information to start the process.

## Networking

A great referral method is networking. There are lots of ways to do this, with entire books available on the subject. Think of networking as a public relations campaign for yourself. You want your name and reputation to circulate among as many people as possible. If someone mentions they're in the market for what you sell, one of your network contacts will pass your name on to them or let you know that person is in the market. If you're lucky, you might even get an endorsement along with the lead.

Good networkers go to lots of meetings, actively belong to many organizations, and work at the process in an organized fashion. They don't just let it happen. Needless to say, they always have a supply of business cards on hand, are alert to all potential prospects, and they always reciprocate.

Remember that successful networking requires a conscious effort on your part. It's one of those tasks that easily gets pushed aside by more pressing business. It's easy to skip a couple of meetings because you got too busy, or put off those networking phone calls you were going to make because you had paperwork that had to get done. It's tempting to rely on happenstance to produce networking opportunities. But the best salespeople are proactive and generate the opportunities themselves.

It's a good idea to budget some time for it. Set aside a specific hour every week (outside prime selling time) to go through your

## CARD TRICKS

Business cards don't do any good hiding in your desk—they're only useful when they're spread around. Here are some ideas to get them into circulation:

○ Don't hand out just one card. Make it a practice to give two and ask the recipient to pass the extra one on to someone else.

○ Give one to the customer on every call, not just the first one. Ask them to pass them on.

○ Give one to every person in a group presentation, not just the decision maker.

○ Give a card to every receptionist when you ask to see the prospect.

○ Put two cards in the envelope with every letter, birthday card or thank you note.

Rolodex and call 10 people just to say hello and see how they are getting along. When you see an acquaintance's name in a trade journal, drop her a short note. Every quarter, send a business card and brochure to everyone on your Christmas card list. Include a short note asking them to do you a favor and pass the brochure along to anyone they know who might benefit from your services or products. You never know.

# COMPETITIVE MONITORS

The prospecting method most commonly used in many industries is monitoring the competition. There are even companies that provide this service for a fee. At most companies, however, the salespeople find it in their job descriptions. In some industries, the users of the product or service are known publicly. For example, if you sell car fleet leasing services, you can identify which companies lease from your competitors by examining state car registration records. If you're in the ad sales business, you can readily see the prospects who advertise on the competitive media.

A truly aggressive salesperson will make it a practice to religiously monitor competitive activity. Make it a habit to know who is using your competitor's products so that you have a ready source of leads.

# QUALIFYING LEADS

In some industries, the prospect list is provided to you or is readily apparent. For example, if you sell prescription drugs, your list of prospects consists primarily of the licensed physicians in your territory since they have to approve your product's purchase before the end user can buy it.

If you sell a service like direct-mail advertising, however, any business that you can contact is prospect. That's a large list, consisting of approximately every business with a telephone or mailing address in the world. What you need is a way to cull that list down to the most promising names.

This part of the prospecting process is the qualifying step. Think of it as pouring gravel through a series of successively smaller grid screens. You start with a large, mixed up mess going into the first screen and end up with a few pieces exactly the right size. The information you have or can get about each prospect dictates whether they can go through each screen.

The methods I've discussed are all designed to put a lot of gravel into your screen. They generate leads. But leads and prospects are two different things. Leads are suspects, not prospects, until you determine whether they are capable of buying your product or service.

## A Common Sense Approach

You also need to screen them on the probability of their purchasing from you. That's why competitive monitors work so well—the prospect demonstrates a willingness and ability to buy something like your product. To narrow the list of prospects down, you need to qualify them in some (or many) ways. But watch out, qualifying has a lot of pitfalls.

My first sales manager, a man in a plaid sport coat whom I considered to be a sales god, used to say, "Pick the cherries that are ripe," which, of course, meant to call on those prospects who were most likely to buy at a given time. Almost every product or service has a seasonal or cyclical factor that dictates the timing of a prospect's needs. You can postpone out-of-season prospects and concentrate on those most likely to buy today.

Another produce-related axiom he often used was "Go after the low-hanging fruit." It's more efficient to sell the easiest prospects than the hard ones—the fruit that grows highest on the tree. This made sense at the time, particularly since it told me not to work as hard.

The pitfall in both these approaches, however, is that each of my competitors was doing the same thing. Everybody was going after the easy pickings, to use one last fruit adage.

I stepped back and realized that these prospects were current users of my or my competitors' products (which is why I knew their buying cycle) and they were easy to sell—and to switch pitch—because they based their decisions mostly on price. This was easy to do since all of us were competing for the same business.

I finally learned to devote enough time to get my share of these prospects, but to devote the bulk of my *creative* selling efforts to finding and qualifying prospects the competition hadn't gotten to yet. These prospects were the ones who made it hard to get in to see the decision maker, or didn't appear to have much potential, or somehow otherwise discouraged my competitors. I suspected that some of those prospects had big potential—and I was right.

## Assumptions

Many times you disqualify a prospect based on assumptions. You jump to a conclusion based on your suppositions, not research. As a consequence, you don't have enough hard data to make a decision.

Additionally, if prospects don't use a product sold by you or your competitors, you assume there must be a reason and don't pursue it. Sometimes there is a good reason they don't buy, but often the situation becomes a classic self-fulfilling prophecy. Since no one is trying to sell them, they don't buy. Since they don't buy, you don't try to sell them.

Or you make assumptions based on incorrect information. For example, you look at prospects' buildings or neighborhoods and assume they don't have much potential. By not calling on them, you may be missing a great opportunity. Never assume anything.

I used to travel a two-lane highway that ran between two good customers located in towns about 30 miles apart. I sold TV advertising at the time. About midway between my two customers was a small farmhouse with a metal machine shed behind it. It looked like a dozen other farmhouses with sheds just like it on that highway, except that this house had a sign out front that said "Energy Savers" on it. I probably drove by that house and its sign for six months.

Finally, my curiosity got the best of me and I was ahead of schedule, so I stopped to see just what "Energy Savers" was all about. I knocked on the front door of the house and got no answer. I walked around to the back and heard somebody whistling in the machine shed. When I went inside, I found a big guy in overalls lying under a trailer working to get a piece of baling wire unwound from one of the axles. He didn't look like the normal TV advertiser.

But it turned out he not only became a TV advertiser, but he became one of my largest accounts! Like many farmers, he had a business on the side. "Energy Savers" turned out to be an early provider of blown insulation, which offered an inexpensive, nonintrusive way to insulate the side walls and ceilings of homes. It was a perfect product to advertise on television and because it carried such a high profit margin, the guy in the overalls bought a lot of TV advertising from me.

If I judged the potential by the appearance of the prospect, I never would have made that first call. Remember, you can't deposit assumptions in your bank account—only commissions.

Prospecting shouldn't be a chore. It is the beginning of the Creative Selling System, when you open your mind to possibilities and try to make them happen. It's one more adventure in selling.

# CHAPTER 14

# IF IT FEELS GOOD, DO IT AGAIN

nd now, just to thoroughly confuse the issue, let's talk about the importance of repeat business. I know, I know—I've spent the entire book looking at ways to sell new customers. But let's assume for a moment you plan on having your job or business next year, too. If so, you must devote a significant amount of time to growing your revenue from current customers.

Current customers are your best source of new business. They know you, they know your product, they have demonstrated a willingness to purchase. What's more, you know them, you've learned about their needs, and you've invested a significant amount of time in the success of their business. Protect that investment and encourage it to grow the same way you manage your investment portfolio, making adjustments periodically to maximize your return.

Current customers are also your company's most profitable customers. The heavy start-up costs were already absorbed and written off. The current customers have passed the credit checks, had their account data fed into your computer, been educated about your billing practices, learned how to use your customer support and service staffs, and otherwise incurred the typical back office cost necessary to start doing business with a new account.

They've probably also passed the most expensive stage of incurring initial selling costs. You've used the get-acquainted offer, the short-term trial contract, and the sales promotion expense to bring them into the company. You've done your basic research, invested your time in preparing the initial proposals, tracked down the decision makers, and made all the follow-up presentations to make the first sale. Generally, you don't have to do these things again.

Concentrate on keeping current customers happy and increasing your business with them while you develop new accounts. To build a successful account list or territory, you have to do both tasks. There is no rest in sales unless you decide you're not going to grow your business. If that's your decision, you'll have plenty of time to rest—in line at the unemployment office.

# CUSTOMERS FOR LIFE

Try to turn all customers into customers for life. Bowl them over with your service. Become such an integral part of their companies that you have your own desk in their offices. Develop solutions before they even discover a need.

You won't have a lifelong relationship with many customers, but when you do, you'll profit from it. I have a handful of customers with whom I've done business for many years at more than one company, including my own. A few represent millions of dollars in income over the years. You can enjoy the same kind of long-term relationship with your best customers if you never stop selling them.

They may become your friends. They may rely on your service or products to the exclusion of all others. They may tell you that they'll always be your customers and sign long-term contracts to prove it. But if you take them and their business for granted, you'll regret it someday.

## Never Stop Selling

You'll also be sorry if you rely on them as your main income source. Having one dominant customer is dangerous because there are too many variables outside your control—and theirs. "For life" is a long, long time.

Situations and people change. The foundation of a wonderful relationship two years ago may not mean anything today. Your relationship with a life customer is similar to a marriage. The relationship must evolve to stay vibrant, alive and satisfying to both of you.

## How Much Is That Customer In The Window?

Acquiring a new customer doesn't come cheaply. There are many costs incurred after you land a new account—most of them in the form of time used for the following seven procedures:

1. Credit checks

2. Establishment of payment terms

3. Internal accounting setup

4. Internal shipping department setup

5. Customer indoctrination and training

6. Salesperson handholding

7. Management monitoring

To get a good idea of the costs to your company, ask every department what they do when an order comes in from a new customer. You might be surprised at how much goes on behind the scenes.

So never stop selling them. Every time your company comes out with a new product or service, pitch it to your current customers first. If it's really a new-and-improved model, don't you owe it to them? If there's a limited supply, shouldn't your best customers get first shot at it?

Always add value to their current purchases. If your company offers an inducement to new customers, shouldn't your loyal customers get the same deal? It's a real slap in the face if they don't. If the new business incentive is a small price to pay for a new account, it's an even smaller price to pay to keep a current one. That's one of the management dilemmas behind sales promotions.

# SALES PROMOTIONS

One of the persistent bad practices in the advertising sales business is to offer "incentive travel" to new advertisers spending a minimum amount or to current advertisers who increase their spending by a similar amount.

Those who qualify typically get a free trip for two to some vacation spot where they travel with the TV or radio station management and the other advertisers who qualified. Many other businesses offer similar incentive promotions to generate quick revenues.

This type of sales promotion always seems to generate loads of "new revenue" the first year it's run. Of course, there's no way of knowing whether the customers would have spent that money anyway, if the sales effort had been as intense. All the station knows is that the travel promotion "generated new revenue."

Since it worked the first time, you do it again, right? The second year, however, you're faced with a dilemma. What's the threshold for qualifying for a trip? Those "new accounts" who signed on last year now have to increase their spending significantly to qualify because these trips aren't cheap. And the long-term customers have to do the same. The third year the problem gets worse.

> If you're going to reward a customer for doing business with you, shouldn't you reward the most profitable customer first?

It doesn't take the advertisers long to figure out that they can ensure getting a trip every other year if they cut their spending during alternate years because the spending minimums are always based on a previous period's spending! So the broadcaster enjoys a real roller-coaster ride as their long-term customers take advantage of the "new business" promotion.

Should the broadcaster avoid that problem by offering the trip only to new customers? They can, but what kind of message does that send to long-term advertisers about how much the station values their business? Not a positive one. If you're going to reward a customer for doing business with you, shouldn't you reward the most profitable customer first? A new account is never as profitable as an existing one of equal size, anyway.

These types of sales promotions are losing favor in many fields. There's been a decided swing away from sales promotion spending, which generates only short-term sales, and toward advertising spending, which establishes loyalty and repeat sales as well as immediate sales.

# Price Promotion And Market Share

The most popular type of sales promotion is the price promotion. Like the rationale for nearly every sales promotion, price promotion is justified on the grounds that it builds market share. That's only true in the most superficial sense. It's an illusion that will disappear tomorrow.

The purpose behind building market share is to increase the base of brand-loyal customers who will make future purchases without incurring further sales promotion expense. In other words, today's market share has no value if it is not an indicator of tomorrow's.

I'll do a little math to illustrate the point. Here's the situation: Your product costs $10 to make and you normally sell it for $15, making a $5 profit. I'm going to keep it simple by assuming that you have one customer who buys it once per quarter (four times per year), so your gross profit is $20 per year. Now let's do some sales promotion to increase your market share.

"Attention Shoppers! For a limited time only, you can buy our product for just $12—you save 20 percent!"

Let's say that the promotional advertising cost is $2 and the discount is $3, so you're selling your product at cost to build share.

The response is great. You get another customer right away (doubling your market share!). Of course your existing customer also pays the lower price, so you've effectively doubled your sales and wiped out your profit for that quarter. It looks like this:

|                    | No Promotion | With Promotion |
|--------------------|:------------:|:--------------:|
| Gross Sales        | $15          | $24            |
| Cost of Goods Sold | $10          | $20            |
| Promotion Expense  | $0           | $4             |
| Gross Profit       | $5           | $0             |

But zero profit is OK because you're building market share for future purchases, right? And those future purchases are supposed to be profitable, am I correct? Which means that both customers will have to pay full price and there will be no promotional spending in subsequent quarters.

Good theory, bad practice. Since new customers are price sensitive (or they would have bought the product without the price cut in the first place), how likely are they to make a subsequent purchase at a higher price? Not very.

What's more, what's going on in the heads of your current customers? Their next purchase will have to be at the original price—which represents a 25 percent increase over the most recent price they paid (the $12 promotional price plus a $3 increase to the $15 original price equals a 25 percent increase). They'd have to be pretty loyal to your brand to put up with that.

The result of this sales promotion is a temporary increase in market share, elimination of profit, and endangering of the current customer relationship.

A better way is to build market share by promoting the *value* of your product, which reinforces the brand loyalty of current customers and attracts new ones (who are not necessarily price sensitive). You still incur the promotional expense but increase profitability with higher margin sales.

Most companies have found that customers who respond to price promotion have little or no loyalty to the product. When a competitor offers a promotional incentive, they switch without thinking about it and the sponsor of the original promotion loses the investment in those customers.

Adopt a similar strategy for growing your business. Offer periodic sales promotions to generate new business, but devote just as much time and effort into advertising to your current customers. "Advertise" by servicing your current accounts, treating them like the valued customers they are. Send the message that you'll never take their business for granted.

# CONTINUAL SELLING

The best way to make sure long-term customers know you're not taking them for granted is to continually sell them. Advertising works best when it's presented constantly. The message and the medium are important, but the repetition of the message—the frequency with which a customer sees the ad—is paramount. Good customer relations are built the same way.

As you practice continual selling, watch out for a few pitfalls. Most businesses encourage long-term orders. A contract to deliver the product or service in increments of several months is considered more valuable than a series of contracts to deliver the same volume written one month at a time. The security of the long-term contract is often so important that the vendor grants a discount or other special terms to the customer. Salespeople recognize the value because they know that it's more efficient to sell one contract than 12.

But there's a downside to long-term contracts. Some salespeople believe they've secured all the business they're going to get from the customer who signs a contract, so they stop selling the customer until that contract is up for renewal. In some cases, the customer won't even hear from the salesperson until it's time to renew. This attitude not only impairs the relationship with the customer, but it also blinds the salesperson to many good opportunities.

I'm sure that your company has a continuous stream of new products, repackaged lines, sales promotions, and maybe even a price change or two. The first place you should sell these is among your current customers. They've already shown their willingness to buy from you, so keep the boiler stoked by continually feeding it new fuel.

Your customer's needs may have changed since that long-term contract was signed. The contract may have left some money on the table or there may be a "contingency fund" in the customer's budget, held back for last-minute opportunities. You'll never know unless you constantly offer additions to the contract.

Another advantage of continual selling is that you are always trying out new ideas on your customers. You get all those great idea selling advantages, not the least of which is frequent feedback on what they like and don't like, need and don't need. Whether you sell any add-ons or not, this is very useful information at renewal time.

# CONTRACT RENEWAL STRATEGY

Contract renewals are far from automatic, even with your very best customers. That's why you should develop a renewal strategy that's as complete as your plan for selling a new major account.

First, when you start working on a renewal, move the decision date earlier every time. It helps fend off your competitors. Just as you monitor your competition, they're also monitoring your accounts, waiting for the opportunity to steal your biggest account at renewal time.

The best way to foil their attack is to preclude it by locking up the renewal early. If you wait for the prospect to tell you it's time for renewal, it's too late. You should be the proactive party in the transaction.

Do your estimate (or re-estimate) of their spending potential, study their needs as you now know them, and put that proposal for the renewal on the table as early as you can. At best, you have a good chance of getting an early renewal. At worst, you set the standards for the competition. It's generally better to defend your position than assault someone else's.

## Setting Renewal Goals

When renewal time rolls around, make sure you set your sights high enough. Don't limit your expectations by the size of the last contract.

Salespeople often stereotype current customers into boxes—and the size of the box is not based on their total potential as a revenue source but on what they spent with you the first time you sold them.

This system of classification is even worse when you take over an account that had been handled by someone else, like your predecessor in the territory. There's a particular danger of improper classification with some computerized sales automation systems because they can't take into account what should be, only what has been. Many time management systems encourage you to rank your prospects by dollar volume and allocate your time accordingly, compounding the error.

If you sort your customers into boxes based on their previous spending, you're putting yourself into a box, too—a box that limits the potential for growth in your commission check. You should have no more preconceived ideas about current customers than you do about new prospects. Don't let past spending be the sole determinant of the size of future proposals.

Remember that stereotyping works both ways. Just as you've classified the account based on its past spending, the buyer has probably classified you based on the size of your proposals. If you've been selling them small deals, you're grouped with unimportant vendors. If the amount they spend with you moves the needle on their income statement, you'll be in a much larger box.

I recommend periodic reviews of current account potential along the lines of the initial research you did for your new accounts in the Creative Selling System. There's no law that says you can't do the same kind of research with your current accounts. In fact, you're doing your customers a real service if you take the time to analyze them that way.

Start with a fresh needs analysis, as if you were getting ready to pitch a new account—then add the knowledge you've gained during the term of the current contract. Has the competitive scene changed? Has the customer made any changes? The list of questions is endless, but they should all give you a clearer map of the route to a sizable renewal.

Next, look outside the box and estimate their revenue potential using the methods I've already covered. If there's a discrepancy between the estimate and their actual spending, you may have identified an opportunity.

## Renew With Ideas

But above all, don't forget the idea! A good creative seller bases the renewal proposal on a fresh idea. Since you now know the customer's business intimately, your ideas should be real barn-burners.

Idea power works on renewal customers the same way it works on new prospects. It firmly establishes you as a resourceful ally. It separates you from the competition. It moves you and your proposal further up the decision-making chain. But don't forget the key advantage of idea selling, which is its focus on value rather than price.

> Don't forget the key advantage of idea selling, which is its focus on value rather than price.

A typical contract renewal usually starts with you deciding how much more to ask the account to spend. That amount is generally determined by the budgeted revenue increase your company imposed on your sales manager or associate, and has nothing to do with customers' needs.

Look at what the customer spent last year, what prices were paid for what inventory or services, and you put together a proposal for the same thing with an additional item or two, plus some unit price increases. Sound familiar?

When you pitch this insightful piece of work to the customer, he will consider it with two things in mind:

1. "Since this is the same thing I bought last year, am I satisfied enough with it to buy it again?

2. "And if I buy it again, can I get a lower price?"

Then he'll pull out the proposal your competition made and compare prices. Since the competition had a year to study what your customer bought from you, they've undoubtedly offered their version of it at a lower price. Even if they haven't, your customer will say they have.

The customer also informs you that he wasn't entirely happy with what you sold him last year and has to have a better price this year to justify buying the same thing again. Since you have no argument, you have to negotiate the renewal on price.

But what if you had followed the Creative Selling System to set up your renewal pitch? You'd be presenting a new idea to the customer rather than the same old thing. Since your idea is based on the intimate understanding of his needs, it should be right on target. Can he compare your new proposal with the competition's? They came in with last year's model while you presented a com-

## WHICH STRATEGY WOULD YOU CHOOSE?

|  | Standard Renewal | Idea-based Renewal |
|---|---|---|
| ○ Avoids price discussion | No | Yes |
| ○ Can't directly compare previous price | No | Yes |
| ○ Can't compare with competitor prices | No | Yes |
| ○ Avoids false complaints | No | Yes |
| ○ Shows customers you're not taking them for granted | No | Yes |
| ○ Encourages review of your product's ○ benefits | Maybe | Yes |
| ○ Recognizes customers' new needs | No | Yes |
| ○ Shows customers you're still eager to help | No | Yes |

pletely redesigned, up-to-date, forward-looking alternative. Which looks better?

How about comparing the new proposal with the old contract? If the customer says he wasn't satisfied with the old deal, he's playing right into your hands. Once again, what you offer isn't the old deal—it's something new. He can't compare prices—it's apples to kumquats.

# UNHAPPY CUSTOMERS

There's another reason to continually sell current customers. If you don't, you may not know they're unhappy until it's too late.

I shudder when salespeople say that their job is getting the order and it's another department's job to service it. This attitude says that their company experiences a huge amount of account turnover. Most unhappy customers don't complain on their own initiative— they just go elsewhere. If you only see customers when it's time to renew the contract, you may not have been around enough to hear the complaints.

If you rely on the service department to tell you when a customer's unhappy, you're living in a dream world. They don't have time for that—they have customers to service. They don't get paid the big bucks like you, anyway. What do you care if the customer's not happy? They get paid the same whether there's one customer or 20. Shortsighted? Maybe—but true, just the same.

If you are on your customers' doorsteps every week or so trying to sell an addition to their current contract or order, you'll hear if they're unhappy. Wouldn't you rather know now while you can do something about it? If you wait until renewal time, they could end up stewing about the problem for months. Which way gives you the clearer path to renewal?

There's a lot of work to this creative selling thing, isn't there? New accounts, current accounts, prospecting, researching, writing proposals, practicing presentations. I haven't even talked about reports, meetings, training, and other nuisances. How do you get them all done and still have a life?

Read on. The next chapter is about building your personal worth through management of your most valuable asset—your time.

# CHAPTER 15

# YOUR MASTERPIECE IS YOU

Our founding fathers said that all men are created equal. They made two mistakes with that statement. For one, they didn't include women, and two, they didn't take into account that every person is exactly the same in only one respect: We each get 24 hours in every day. The different ways you spend those 24 hours determine how you grow your personal worth.

Many of us think of money as the measure of our personal worth. But personal worth is certainly not just about monetary wealth. There are many other valuable things that don't carry a monetary value: relationships with family and friends, the development of artistic and athletic skills, your accumulation of knowledge, and the growth of your religious or spiritual faith. These things take time. Making money also consumes a lot of your time, so plan for it accordingly.

Time is one of your most valuable assets, so manage it to produce the greatest return on your investment. That return may be in the form of greater income, or it may mean more time to spend with your family. But the principle is the same: Treat your time like any other asset. Don't waste it; capitalize on it.

Sales (especially commission sales) is one of the few occupations where you can see a direct and immediate return on your invested time. In fact, the single most important factor in sales success is how salespeople invest their time. The best and the brightest don't waste a moment. Even salespeople who lack good presentation skills can make up for it by using their time efficiently. On the opposite end of the scale, the floundering salesperson invariably has problems with time management.

# FACE CALLS

There's a simple principle involved in time management for salespeople. More calls means more sales. As Woody Allen said, "Eighty percent of success is being there." You're "there" more often when you make more calls. If you learn nothing more than that from this book, you're ahead of the game.

Let's define a term here. A "call" is a face-to-face meeting where you ask a prospect to buy something. It's not a telephone call to get an appointment or a service call on a current customer. These are important activities, but when I talk about making more calls in the context of business-to-business sales, I'm talking about asking for more orders *in person*.

There is no substitute for meeting with the client in person. When you're there face to face, you build trust. It's really hard to believe in what your customers are saying if you can't look into their eyes while they're saying it. If you've done any telephone sales, you know how hard it is to create a trusting relationship with a prospect who can't see you.

You also demonstrate your professionalism and transmit your enthusiasm much better in person. "Seeing is believing" is more than just a cliché when it's applied to a sales call. You gain tremendous credibility when prospects see your animation, preparation and control of the presentation. When you're face to face, you focus more on the client, which in turn makes your presentation more persuasive.

Personal calls also show prospects you care enough about the success of their business to invest some of your own valuable time into it.

Technological advances have made things easier. You have the fax machine, e-mail, cellular phones, overnight delivery, voice mail, and all kinds of other ways to communicate with your prospects. These high-tech wonders can make you more efficient. But they can't take the place of the face-to-face call. Use modern technology to get more face time with more prospects and current customers. That's where its real value lies.

## Efficiency And Effectiveness

It sounds like I'm pushing you to work harder, doesn't it? Add a couple more hours to your 12-hour workday and you'll make more money. Of course, you may lose a spouse or a couple of kids in the process, but hey, that's just part of the price you pay. More calls means more hours, right? Not necessarily.

I'm not advocating that you work longer hours. I'm suggesting that you find ways to work more efficiently. You can make more calls and work no harder if you improve your efficiency and you can make more sales on those calls if you improve your effectiveness.

Here are three steps for improving time management:

1. Set priorities
2. Plan activities
3. Execute effectively

There are many tools available to help you do these things, from computerized calendars and contact management software to personal coaching and time management seminars. Ultimately, time management is just like any other skill: It can't be taught. It has to be learned by practice.

Time management is about mutually exclusive choices. You can only do one thing at a time. You can't be in two places at the same time. No matter how you express it, you have to choose which account to call on at a particular point in time, and you have to choose what you're going to do on that call. That's what priorities are all about.

In sales, there are two sets of priorities: account priorities and activity priorities. The relationship between the two—how you manage your activities to produce the greatest revenue from the chosen accounts—determines your success.

# ACTIVE ACCOUNT PRIORITIES

Account priorities are pretty straightforward. Which prospect has the potential to yield the greatest revenue for the amount of time invested? Start by quantifying the importance of each current account. In most businesses, the major accounts count and they count big. That's where the popular "80/20" rule came from.

You'd like to give your full attention and top notch service to every account. But in reality, time constraints force you to make choices about how much time and what type of service you render.

Assign priorities to each of your active accounts, based on their potential for contribution to the revenue stream, and divide them into three groups.

## Must-Have Accounts

Must-have accounts are just what their name implies. They represent such a large share of your total business that you must have them or your business's very existence may be jeopardized. In the chart below, the top five accounts represent 26 percent of the company's total revenues. On average, any one of them would be about 5 percent. If your company's net profit margin after taxes is less than 5 percent (which would not be unusual in many industries), the loss of any one of these top five accounts could push your income statement into red ink territory.

---

### YOU'RE THE TOP

Here's a typical breakdown of the contribution various-sized accounts make to a year's revenue for one of my clients:

| | |
|---|---|
| Five Largest Accounts | 26 % of total revenue |
| Next Five Accounts | 10 % |
| Next Five Accounts | 9 % |
| Next Five Accounts | 7 % |
| Total of 20 Largest Accounts | 52 % of total annual revenue |

My client does business with about 350 different accounts every year, but more than half the revenue comes from 20 of them—and less than half comes from all of the other 330 of them!

In other words, major accounts are the lifeblood of every business.

---

I once had a sales position where I handled about 50 different accounts, but two particularly large ones were crucial. The commission on one was large enough to make my mortgage payment each month and the other basically paid the rest of the household bills. I was in deep trouble if either one of them cut back their spending or canceled their contract.

## Priority Accounts

The second group for current accounts are priority accounts. These are fairly large accounts but have the potential to spend a lot more—to become, in essence, must-have accounts. In "You're The Top" on page 196, the accounts ranked 6 through 20 would fall into this category. These accounts are important, but not crucial to your company's survival.

The true importance of priority accounts lies in their potential. They deserve more of your time and effort because they could be much larger contributors to the revenue stream. Also, because they are active accounts, they are often the most fertile ground in which to plant new business seeds. They're profitable, they know you and your company's products, and they can grow if you give them a reason to.

## Other Active Accounts

The third group is simply other active accounts. These are the accounts that do business with you but have limited growth potential. They may be small businesses that don't have the capital to grow or large businesses with a use for only a limited number of your products or services. They may be seasonal accounts. For whatever reason, other active accounts don't have a lot of growth potential.

You can't ignore them because they can represent a significant portion of your total business. The key to efficiently servicing these accounts is not to go off on nonproductive tangents. Stick to the business at hand.

# NEW ACCOUNT PRIORITIES

The only account priority groups I've discussed are current accounts, but you have to give priority to developing new accounts as well or your business will stagnate. In fact, I suggest you place a priority on new accounts equal to that you give to existing ones. It's the only way to make sure you give them the attention they deserve. Again, I'm going to divide the prospects into three groups.

## Target Accounts

These are prospects who have the economic potential to be must-have accounts but who, for one reason or another, don't spend any money with you now. Maybe you sell widgets and they are dedicated wodget users. Maybe your largest competitor has a deep consultive relationship with them. Or maybe no one in your company has yet found the magic button that will convert the target account from a prospect to a customer.

> What you have to do is dedicate yourself (and your time) to stop dreaming about that sale and make it happen.

You know who your target accounts are. Most good salespeople have a couple of dream sales they'd like to make and they're usually to the great big accounts that no one else has been able to sell. You not only get rich from them, but you become famous in the sales annals. What you have to do is dedicate yourself (and your time) to stop dreaming about that sale and make it happen.

There is usually at least one major obstacle to selling the target account. If it were easy, it would have already been done. Setting a high priority on getting the company's business—the same time priority you dedicate to working with a must-have account—is the only way to succeed.

## Unknown Potential Accounts

The next group of prospects is the "unknown" category. I use that name because you don't know their actual potential. Maybe they are new businesses in town or they have new owners. For whatever reason, you don't really know their potential, so your first priority with them is to find out. Since you already know what the potential revenue is from a target account, you have to rank them slightly lower.

All other prospects make up your final group. These accounts are the ones that you are pretty sure will fall into the other active category when they are sold. They'll be small accounts for the same reasons, and you'll assign them the same area on the list of priorities.

# ACTIVITY PRIORITIES

Setting priorities for coverage of your accounts is only half of the process. The other half is determining the priorities of the things you do every day. You can set activity priorities according to the revenue potential of those activities. In general, time spent making face-to-face calls should carry the highest priority while time spent performing nonsales tasks should carry the lowest.

In my time management plan, there are six activity priorities to consider. The highest is making sales calls, or asking someone to buy something from you. As I mentioned earlier, this means face-to-face calls where you lay out a specific proposal to a prospect. These may be cold-calls on new prospects or renewal calls on current customers—or any call where you make a specific proposal. If you are very lucky and well organized, you can spend 60 percent of your average workday selling this way.

## Service Calls

The next highest priority is assigned to service calls. These are face-to-face meetings with current customers that take care of their order in some way. For example, if you sell retirement plans, you may need to spend time with your customer's controller, setting up the payroll withholding procedures. That's time out of your day— maybe a big chunk of time, in fact—that I classify as a service call because the sale has already been made.

Service calls have the second highest priority because of their value in customer retention. Remember, keeping existing customers is just as important and generally more profitable than selling new ones. Servicing customers well is the most reliable way to keep them.

## Preparation For Calls

The third activity priority goes to preparation for sales calls. The Creative Selling System requires a fair amount of research, proposal writing, and presentation rehearsal.

# THE ACCOUNT/ACTIVITY MATRIX

When you relate each activity priority to an account priority, you can fine-tune your workday and maximize the return on your time investment. Here's a matrix that shows how the two sets of priorities relate to each other.

**Activity Priority**

| | Nonsales | Sales Support | Service Prep | Sales Prep | Service Call | Sales Call |
|---|---|---|---|---|---|---|
| Must Have | $ | $ | $ | $ | $ | $ |
| Priority | $ | | $ | $ | $ | $ |
| Target (New) | $ | | | $ | | $ |
| Unknown (New) | | | | $ | | $ |
| Other Active | | | $ | $ | $ | $ |
| Other (New) | | | | $ | | $ |

*(left axis label: Account Priority)*

The closer to the upper right-hand corner your activity falls, the greater the amount of potential revenue. Everything you do with a must-have account is dollar-related, even nonsales activities. Things like social affairs, golf outings, and thank-you lunches with the must have, priority and target accounts personnel fall into this box.

Also notice that every sales call has revenue potential, which ultimately puts it ahead of any nonrevenue-producing activity.

The way to use this chart is to examine your plan each day and ask yourself where on the matrix each intended action falls. Schedule the ones with dollar signs first, so if you run out of time, the nondollar-producing items are held over to the following day.

Some consider this an overly simplistic approach to sales time management, but it drives home the point that sales time is an asset like gold—and needs to be protected accordingly.

The fourth item on the activity priority list is preparation for service calls. Someone (you) has to spend some time in the office getting the materials together for your meetings with the current customers.

## Sales Support

The fifth activity priority is sales support or administrative activities. Sales meetings. Reports. Revenue projections. More sales meetings. Training. All of these things take a bite out of your daily time allotment. If you don't set and observe a priority for them, they'll eat your day alive.

The last priority goes to nonsales activities—those things you need to do sometime during the daylight hours that aren't related to your job, such as personal errands, lunch breaks, etc.

# MAKE A PLAN

"Plan your work and work your plan"—it's a good sales adage because it describes the essence of sound time management. It's not enough to lay out a plan; you have to execute it to get any benefit from it. In fact, if you don't "work your plan," you wasted the time it took to draw it up.

You can spend a lot of time planning. You can also invest hundreds of dollars in account management software and cross-indexed

---

### THE REAL SALES DAY

| | |
|---|---|
| 8 a.m. – 9:30 a.m. | Arrive at office, attend meetings, organize day, leave for first call |
| 9:30 a.m. – 12 p.m. | Prime sales time |
| noon – 1:30 p.m. | Lunch, return phone calls, paperwork, leave for calls |
| 1:30 p.m. – 4:30 p.m. | Prime sales time |
| 4:30 p.m. – 6 p.m. | Return to office, return phone calls, attend meetings, paperwork |

leather-bound time management systems. Or you can make up a "to do" list on a napkin at the coffeeshop. I suggest trying something in-between.

You need both long- and short-term plans. You can call them strategic and tactical plans, if you like military terms. Which is more important? Neither. They serve two distinct, equally important purposes.

## Long-Term Planning

An annual plan is your long-term strategy. It generally includes activities with accounts with the greatest revenue potential. If you don't set time blocks aside for these accounts, the long-term campaign to sell the target account gets pushed aside in the daily rush to get everything else done. But the target accounts—and must-have and priority accounts as well—are too important to overlook.

I use one of those great big wall calendars so I can see all 365 days at once. You may prefer a computerized system or a day-timer. At the beginning of each year, I note when I expect to make presentations to my must-have, priority, and target accounts. There may be one such presentation each month for each account. I mark that 12 times for each one on the calendar.

I then note predictable sales events and sales support activities. These include trade shows and conventions, promotion campaigns, special seasonal offers, sales meetings, and report due dates.

After that, I plug in my vacation (yes—it's important, too) and important personal dates like the kids' school programs, anniversaries, and other things that I don't want to forget in the rush of business. These may be nonsales activities, but if they're valuable, they deserve a place in the plan. If you laid out the first two categories ahead of these, you won't have to worry about being on a fishing trip in Manitoba when your top account's contract comes up for renewal.

## Long-Term Planning Advantages

Having a long-term plan allows me to schedule time to prepare for each event. If I'm planning on making a presentation to a target account during the first week of May, I know I need to do the research the first week of April, write the proposal the second week,

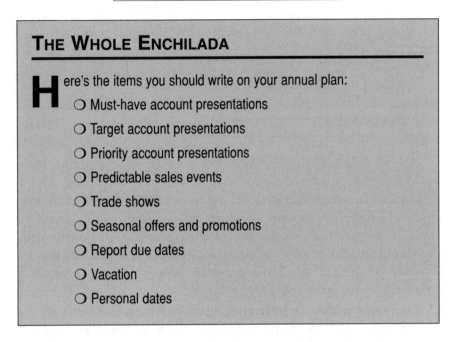

## THE WHOLE ENCHILADA

**H**ere's the items you should write on your annual plan:

- ○ Must-have account presentations
- ○ Target account presentations
- ○ Priority account presentations
- ○ Predictable sales events
- ○ Trade shows
- ○ Seasonal offers and promotions
- ○ Report due dates
- ○ Vacation
- ○ Personal dates

call the prospect for an appointment the third week, and rehearse the presentation the fourth week. If there are other people in the company who play a part in this pitch, they have a timetable as well.

Expect long-term plans to change. Review your annual plan every month and make the necessary adjustments. Lots of things can happen in a year—priorities change.

One advantage of long-term planning (and even short-term) is that it reduces stress. Few things cause higher blood pressure than "discovering" that a report is due tomorrow—and you need some information from a co-worker who left on vacation yesterday. Life is full of such surprises. Planning lowers your stress level and helps you cope better with them.

## Short-Term Planning

The basic tactical tool of the Creative Selling System is the weekly plan. This is where you allocate your time assets in detail so that the annual plan becomes real and the events on it actually occur. I suggest you prepare a weekly plan every Friday (during nonsales time, of course). Again, you can use the format of your choice, but I use a very simple three-column sheet of lined paper. Each column is pretty self-explanatory:

| Account | Idea | Result |
|---------|------|--------|
|         |      |        |
|         |      |        |
|         |      |        |

The middle column, the "Idea," is there to remind you to have an idea for every sales call you make. Whether you're presenting a full-blown five-page Creative Selling System pitch or a quick-and-dirty add-on to an existing contract, this column reminds you to build your proposal around an idea based on a prospect need. Attaching an idea to every planned account call also reminds you to prepare for the call, not just try to wing it on your good looks and glib tongue. It's great self-discipline.

Start the weekly plan by listing annual activities. Look on that big wall calendar and see what's there. List those activities first on the form so you remember to do them first. You'll probably find that there's some activity for your must-have, priority and target accounts on the plan every week. That's as it should be. If they're going to represent 80 percent of your business, they deserve at least that much of your time. Finally, list all the other accounts you want to see and the ideas you're going to pitch them.

## Using Your Weekly Plan

Keep your plan by your side throughout the week, noting in the "Results" column the outcome of your calls so that you know what you have to do to follow up on them and which accounts you need to see the following week. Every Friday, start a new plan by carrying over the calls that didn't get made or require some follow-up. If you like statistics, compile the results of several weeks' plans and look for trends in your performance.

The goal of any time management system should be to produce more revenue, not more reports. That's why I rely on just two pieces of paper—the annual plan and the weekly plan—to cover strategic and tactical plans. You can certainly do more, but beware of becoming plan-bound, when you spend so much time and energy making plans, you never get any actual work done.

One symptom of overplanning is when you make up a "to do" list in the morning with "Make To Do List" at the top of the page. That gives you an item to check off as soon as you're done making the list. It may give you a sense of accomplishment, but I think it's overkill.

# Call Reports

I've always questioned the usefulness of post-call reports, which are nothing more than reports to management on what you did all day. As a stand-alone procedure they take up time better spent working on an activity with future benefits, rather than reporting on something that's already done.

In their worst manifestation, the sales manager (or the poor administrative assistant) keeps a tally of the number of calls, sales, presentations, etc., and calculates a bunch of performance ratios. This gives the sales manager a club to "motivate" the salesperson.

At their best, call reports are a source of market information for sales managers and those above them, but this function is better accomplished in other ways.

## HOW MUCH IS ENOUGH?

I can't tell you how many calls you should plan for each week because I don't know how big your territory is or how long your presentations take. But you should set yourself a goal for the number of sales calls you want to make each day.

For my business, I assume about an hour for each presentation, including local travel time. With a five-and-a-half hour sales day, that means I'm able to get in a maximum of five every day. Quite frankly, if I ever got five solid presentations made in a day I'd be ecstatic (and rich). I can't because too many other things get in the way.

But five is a great goal to shoot for, which means I list 25 accounts on my plan each week.

Decide on an appropriate number and prioritize your list. The ones that get canceled should be those with the lowest potential revenue.

The weekly plan treats salespeople as adults, capable of making sound business decisions about their work priorities. It gives them credit for having the same priorities as the company's. The weekly plan also contains all the history you need, which is information about follow-up calls and pending actions. In other words, the weekly plan is designed to improve future sales, not punish past failures.

# PRESERVING YOUR ASSETS

Executing the plan is the final step. The only way you're going to make all those calls during the week is by cutting the waste out of your workday. There are several things you can do.

○ **Delegate work responsibly.** This particularly applies to servicing existing accounts. You have to strike a balance between your need to maintain positive contact with the customer and your need to work on other accounts. It's the "can't be in two places at the same time" problem. If you have support personnel, delegate some work to them.

Don't forget to show your appreciation for the work they do. When they do something extra for one of your customers, do something extra for them. It doesn't have to be monetary. A short note of thanks goes a long way.

○ **Use your nonsales time wisely.** While you may have five and a half hours of selling time every day, that leaves four and a half hours of nonselling time during the normal workday. How are you spending it? Chitchatting about last night's football game? Reading the newspaper? Planning lunch? I've seen plenty of salespeople (and sales managers as well) who start their days that way.

Nonsales time is when you do your prospect research, write your proposals, rehearse your presentations, etc. You must do these things if you're going to be a successful creative seller, and they require time. Sometimes you need to use evening or weekend hours, but a well-organized salesperson *can* get them done during nonsales office time.

This is also a good time to do your call reports, update your expense logs, and complete the general paperwork. If you find yourself filling out a report for your sales manager on Wednesday morning at 10 a.m., you have a time management problem.

○ **Group your calls geographically.** This is common sense. For several years, I lived and sold in a small town where you could drive from one end to the other in 20 minutes. You would think that grouping my calls geographically would have been more trouble than it was worth. But I soon learned that if I had to make that 20-minute drive between every call, I lost time for a sales call for every three calls I made. I spent an hour shuttling between those three calls (20 minutes times three calls equals 60 minutes in the car). This meant about a 25 percent reduction in income! I soon learned to group my calls geographically.

○ **Schedule telephone work for nonsales time.** It's a little easier these days with cellular phones, beepers, and voice mail, but taking and making phone calls eats up a lot of sales time. Consider that time before 9:30 a.m., during lunch, and after 4:30 p.m. as your prime phone time. Your customers are in or around their offices then and so are you, so it's the best time to make telephone contact.

○ **Use voice mail effectively.** Voice mail can be a real time and energy saver. Use voice mail to its best advantage, which is not simply to record your pleas for a return call. Efficient sellers learn to leave informational messages on the recorder so recipients can respond with information of their own.

○ **Work on one thing at a time.** You need to focus on proposals and paperwork during nonsales time. It's hard to do since much of your success depends on the ability to juggle several tasks at once. But "desk work" is different. Failure to concentrate on a task adds significant time to the process and increases the probability of mistakes.

Some things (and people) just take up too much time. To put a spin on an old saying: Change the ones you can, avoid the ones you can't change, and minimize the ones you can't avoid. Here are some common items with large appetites for your time:

○ **Meetings:** Unfortunately, you usually have to go to them. They're important to someone important so that makes them important to you. Do your part to make the meetings useful and efficient. If you can, request that they be scheduled during nonsales time. If you are expected to actively participate, be prepared so you don't spend a lot of time trying to get your act together during the meeting. Don't be the person who talks just to be talking, either. If you have something to contribute, by all means do so, but if you're just talking because you think you're supposed to, you're wasting your time and everybody else's.

○ **Reports:** These fall somewhat into the same category as meetings. Reports bring out the procrastinator in all of us, so do them as quickly and correctly as you can. The best way to handle an unpleasant task is not to put it off and hope it goes away but to exercise personal discipline and *just do it.* Get it over with so you can get to something you really want to do—like making sales calls.

○ **Morning Syndrome:** It afflicts many salespeople. This condition arises when little things command all your attention in the morning, demanding to be finished before you leave the office. So you attend to them. You return that phone call, step down the hall to talk to the production department, take a few moments to straighten your desk—and the next thing you know, it's 10:30 a.m. Guess what? You've lost an hour of prime selling time. If this happens more than once a week, you've got a serious problem.

One cure for this insidious time-stealer is to set an alarm clock

## ON THE CLOCK

To make sure you're always using your time effectively, put this checklist where you'll see it frequently.

❏ Delegate work responsibly.

❏ Use nonsales time wisely.

❏ Group calls geographically.

❏ Schedule phone work.

❏ Use voice mail productively.

❏ Work on one thing at a time.

❏ Minimize meetings.

❏ Control reports.

❏ Avoid Morning Syndrome.

❏ Prioritize emergencies.

❏ Manage pleasant distractions.

for 9:15 a.m. When it goes off, finish whatever you're working on before 9:30, then leave. If you can't finish it, leave anyway and make arrangements to finish it at noon.

If someone comes in to see you after the alarm goes off, say you have a 9:30 appointment and make an appointment with them for later in the day. Don't pick up the phone after 9:15 unless you know the call will take 2 minutes or less. After a few weeks, you'll be surprised at how much earlier you get in front of prospects—and how many more sales you make because you were there.

○ **Putting out fires:** One of the most common time-related job complaints I hear is that emergencies never stop. Entire days are lost as one "critical" situation after another clamors for your attention. Every department in the company brings you a smoldering problem to stamp out.

The next time someone barrels into your office with the latest "emergency," ask if you can get back with him or her at noon because you have an emergency of your own—a customer meeting—at 9:30. Make them take the responsibility for canceling a sales call. Most "emergencies" can hold for a couple of hours and you'll be surprised how many seem to get taken care of before your noon appointment.

○ **Pleasant distractions:** These are time-killers that salespeople are particularly susceptible to. Do you have a chatty customer with whom you've struck up a friendship? It's really easy to slip into his or her office for a few minutes of conversation about last night's TV special. Those few minutes turn into an hour before you know it.

Don't fall into that trap. You should be happy that customers enjoy spending time with you, but remember that you are happier when they spend money with you.

# TIME VALUATION

It may seem obvious, but every minute away from prime selling time costs money. To quantify it, calculate your "sales hourly wage" by dividing your annual income, including commissions by 1,270 hours, which is the approximate number of prime selling hours in a

## BEST LAID PLANS OF MICE AND SALESMEN

Of course, not all time plans work out. One of the exercises I use at time management seminars is to ask everyone in the audience to list everything they did the day before in 15-minute increments from 8 a.m. to 6 p.m. I promise them that no one will see the list but me. I can always tell how honest the group is when I see how much nonsales time they list.

The prize for the most egregiously wasted day goes to three salespeople in Mississippi who collectively spent six hours trying to unlock one car. The salesperson had locked his keys in it when he got to the office that morning. I don't know why it took three of them to get the door unlocked. I'd hate to see them try to change a light bulb.

At least I knew they were honest because nobody would make something like that up.

year. If you gross $63,500 annually, your sales time is worth $50 per hour to you.

I'd be pretty upset if I let a $50 bill fall out of my pocket. But that's the same thing as spending an hour of selling time yakking about the movie you saw last weekend. I'd be even more upset if I spent an hour of selling time writing a proposal. It would be like setting that $50 on fire.

To help practice sound time management, calculate your "sales hourly wage" and write it on the back of a business card. Tape that card someplace time-wasting might occur, like on your telephone or on your steering wheel. Every time you use one of them, you'll be reminded to ask yourself if what you're doing is the best use of your time.

Here's a real eye-opener. Track *everything* you do in 15-minute increments for a week. Add up the actual sales time. Be brutally honest with yourself and *only count sales calls where you asked someone to buy something*. If that time totals less than 27 and a half hours for the week, you've got a time leak someplace.

If you want to really plug that leak, multiply the lost time by your sales hourly wage and then by the 52 weeks in the year. That's the size of the raise you can give yourself if you work at it.

In sales, time is money—your money.

# CHAPTER 16

# THE CREATIVE
# SELLING LIFE

**D**o you remember your very first sales call?

I remember mine very clearly. I can't remember my first sale, but my first sales call is deeply etched into my mind. It was a general debacle as sales calls go, but that first call told me why the sales life was the one for me.

I was an eager lad, not quite old enough to legally order a beer, working as an announcer for my hometown radio station. The general manager of the station called me into his office one day and asked if I wanted to earn some extra money selling advertising for the station on my own time. I could keep my current job and make some money in commissions on the side. What a deal.

He pulled a list of 20 prospects from the phone book, showed me a rate card and told me to go get 'em. The only training he gave me was to say, "Keep asking them to buy until they say 'no' three times, then go on to the next one." This was (and unfortunately still is) pretty standard sales training for the broadcasting industry.

My first call was on a roadside diner in Elwood, Kansas. The only person in the place was a rather large waitress holding a big spatula.

"Excuse me, Miss," I said, "Are you the owner here?"

"Yeah, what do you want?"

"I'd like to offer you some radio advertising today."

"Don't want any. Get out."

"But radio doesn't have to cost a lot of money. . ."

"Don't want none. Get out!"

"Let me show you. . . . "

And that's when she came around the counter taking dead aim at my head with that big spatula, which I assumed was the third "no." I ran for my car.

As soon as my heart stopped thumping, I knew sales was going to be my field. Where else could you get such excitement? Such challenge? Learn so much about other people and human nature and get paid doing it?

That was many years ago, of course, and a lot of things have changed since then. Most things about sales haven't changed, though, and I doubt they ever will.

# WHY SALES?

What attracted me to sales was the freedom the job offered. I could come and go pretty much as I pleased, work on the things I wanted to work on, set my own goals, and use the methods I wanted to achieve them. Of course, I had to make sure these things didn't contradict the company's policies and practices, but that has never been hard since every company I've sold for wanted the same things I did: more sales from more customers. I soon found that if I produced those things, all of us were happy.

But the personal freedom of sales turned out to be just a side benefit. The real source of gratification is personal responsibility. Selling gives you the freedom to set and pursue your own goals, but holds you responsible to yourself for accomplishing them. When salespeople accept that responsibility, they take the first step on the path to satisfaction and success.

Another thing that hasn't changed is the need for salespeople to communicate with prospects. Advancing technology makes some transactional sales functions obsolete, but as long as *people* make the decisions about what to buy, there is an important place for salespeople in our economy.

Selling will always be fun. It combines many positive forces in life: learning new things, facing difficult challenges and meeting a wide variety of people. You get to make a pretty good (or even very good) living, and you can take most of the credit for your success.

Above all, you get to take some interesting risks, which adds plenty of spice to your life.

Creativity is a risk-taking enterprise. Endeavoring to make something new is risky. Risk might be defined as the ability to fail. You may spend hours, days, even weeks on a project but fail to conceive an idea that's workable. Even if you do create one, you may fail to complete it satisfactorily and have to abandon it. Even if your idea comes to fruition, you may fail to find a market for it. Even if you sell it, your idea may not produce the results your customer expected. Every one of these potential failures hurts your ego and your pocketbook. With all these ways to fail, why try?

Because not every idea fails and the ones that succeed reward you tremendously. The risk-reward ratio is actually stacked in your favor. What's even better, you will improve the odds of success as your professional capabilities grow.

## SMALL IDEA = BIG REWARDS

I once represented a TV station in Maine, the state popularly known as "Vacationland" because it attracts millions of visitors every summer. One of my customers was Burger King, which was looking for a promotional vehicle to capture all those tourists visiting the area every summer.

In looking at this opportunity, I remembered that the TV station aired short public-service announcements about upcoming community events—church socials, bean suppers, rummage sales—in unsold ad time throughout the day. We rechristened the announcements "The Burger King Vacationland Bulletin Board" and stuck a Burger King commercial in the middle of each one. Their advertising agency bought it from me on the first presentation. Everyone loved the idea. The TV station moved some unused inventory at premium rates and Burger King got a great tie-in to both the local community and the tourist trade.

My reward came not just in the satisfaction of a job well done and the commissions that went with it, but the sale was considered so creative, it also earned me a large promotion. The rewards from this one sale made up for many, many "failures" and made the risks worthwhile.

## Sales Rewards

Selling has some obvious rewards—good income, the gratification of closing deals and attaining quotas, among others. Good salespeople set their own goals and plan their own rewards. Sure, they may also have company-set quotas and commission plans, but they work to achieve them because the company furthers their opportunity to attain personal goals and receive their rewards.

Star salespeople make their goals tangible: opening 50 new accounts in a year; closing the toughest account in town; owning their own business before they're 30. They don't allow fudge factors, and they don't give rewards to themselves for trying—only for succeeding. When they achieve their goals, they can honestly say "I did it."

I promised myself that the first year I earned $100,000, I would buy a hand-tailored, custom-made Brooks Brothers suit. A salesperson I know gave herself a hiking trip to the floor of the Grand Canyon when she closed her first sale over $500,000. One of the most distinctive rewards I've seen is when a friend pledged that he would quit his job and start his own company after he led his sales team to their fifth record year in a row.

## Set Your Own Rewards

If you don't have tangible goals and rewards, get some. Make a list of things you'd like to have. List everything you can think of—it's OK to put a few "If I Won The Lottery" items on there, too. Do this *first* and get fired up about the possibilities.

Now make a shorter list of goals. There are two tests the goals must pass: 1) They have to be complementary to the goals your company has and 2) they have to just barely be attainable—within reach only if you stand on your tiptoes. Now pick one of those goals—just one—and set a deadline for achieving it.

Finally, pick a reward from your first list. You must be able to give it to yourself when you achieve your goal. A seat on the space shuttle may not pass this test, but a vacation in the Bahamas might. Do whatever it takes to fix these two items in your mind. Write them on an index card and put it in your pocket. Make a screen saver out of them and put it on your computer. The salesperson who went on the hiking trip kept her goal in mind by hanging a picture of the

Grand Canyon over her desk. Do something to keep your goal and your reward dangling in front of you at all times.

# MONEY MOTIVATION

Whenever I'm asked to deliver a seminar on motivation, I always ask whether they really mean motivation or compensation. Most companies confuse the two. They think that the way they pay their

## THE DREAM BOARD

One of my best friends sits down with his wife at New Year's and creates what they call the Dream Board.

The Dream Board is nothing more than a large panel on which they list all the things they want to accomplish during that year. They range from little things like planting a new flowering tree in the backyard, to big ones like getting a Ph.D.

They do this together because they know their chances of success are better if they're both working toward the same goals. Many of the goals are individual, of course, but they also know that supporting each other is one of the many things that makes their marriage work.

To keep the Dream Board from being just another to-do list, they find pictures and objects related to their goals to pin along with the words. They clip these out of magazines and brochures and pin them to the board. To anyone else, it looks like something you'd find in a fifth-grade classroom, but to them it looks just fine.

Many people would consider the Dream Board unsophisticated or immature. I don't because I know what my friends have accomplished in their lives. They retired from the rat race and moved to the place of their dreams before the age of 40. Both started new careers doing things they *wanted* to do rather than things they *had* to do. And he's well on his way to getting that Ph.D.

The Dream Board turns vague desires into concrete achievements.

salespeople will determine how successful those salespeople will be. You and I know that money's only one part of the deal—and one of the smallest parts of all. Motivation is about having goals and rewards in your soul. The money just helps you buy the rewards.

One of the companies I helped start was a nationwide advertising sales organization. I made plenty of mistakes, but I also learned a lifetime of lessons about human nature and motivation. One of the most important things I learned is that the best salespeople aren't motivated purely by money. As a start-up, the company didn't have a revenue stream on which to base commissions, nor did it have the money to promise big signing bonuses or hefty salaries to recruit star salespeople from established competitors.

> One of the most important things I learned is that the best salespeople aren't motivated purely by money.

What I *was* able to promise them was a company built around creative selling. Since the people I recruited were working in an established industry, they didn't have a lot of opportunity for creative selling. In fact, most of the firms they worked for measured a salesperson's success purely by the volume of transactions they could handle. Creativity had very little to do with it.

I believed that a start-up built on creating new opportunities would be successful in that industry. I also knew that to make it successful I needed the best salespeople I could find. I didn't have the time or resources to hire and train rookies, and I knew my concept wouldn't work if I hired anything less than the best.

What I had to offer was the chance to flourish in a very different way—to create sales opportunities rather than process orders. Of course, this meant more work, more risks, and pretty vague monetary rewards compared to what they were doing. I counted on their creative drive to lure them to us.

I was successful in hiring some of the best and the brightest. They weren't necessarily the "top producers" at their old companies, but they were definitely the ones who had the itch to succeed in a creative environment—and they succeeded spectacularly. The company I started went from zero to $35 million in annual sales in the first year—then more than doubled to $75 million in the second. It produced an operating profit in the first year. I also proved that selling in musty old industries could be fun if the job was redefined as a creative enterprise.

What's pertinent about this story is that the company's sales compensation plan was a simple salary. No commissions, no bonuses, no spiffs. The closest thing I had to monetary motivation was the $100 bounty I offered to the salesperson who brought in the new company's first order. The salaries weren't particularly generous. In fact, some of the people I recruited actually took a slight cut in pay to work for the new company. I am convinced that every one of the salespeople succeeded because they were motivated by pride in a job well done.

The story doesn't have a happy ending, though. In our third year, the company came under control of a larger firm, which immediately imposed its commission-based compensation plan on my staff. It may have been coincidental, but sales that year grew at exactly the same rate the rest of the industry was growing.

One by one, the salespeople started drifting away to other opportunities, and the company settled into the same rut as everyone else in the industry. I strongly believe that the average performance was due to salespeople fixated on commission checks rather than personal pride in the job they were doing. The company achieved mediocrity.

## Mediocrity

Be careful. You may only run a company of one (yourself), but the same thing can happen to you. If I had just one piece of advice to give anyone in sales, it would be this: Don't ever settle for mediocrity.

You'll be tempted to allow a little mediocrity to slip in now and then because it takes hard work to be a creative seller. There aren't any magic spells to make it easy, either. If mediocrity has anything going for it, it's that it's easy—but easy things and solid rewards are never connected.

Don't be mediocre. You have a creative spark that will grow into raging excellence if you just fuel it with opportunity and a little work.

## Resolution

Success requires resolution. If you ask my mother why I am a successful salesperson, she'll say it's because I'm stubborn. Maybe she's right. I hope you are resolute—or stubborn—enough to stick to it until you succeed.

Once when I was selling TV advertising, I was assigned an account that every salesperson in the station had handled and failed with at one time or another. It was a furniture store that employed a little advertising agency, mainly to screen out salespeople.

The furniture store spent a grand total of $1,000 on our station every year for as long as records had been kept. Never a penny more. Yet this was the largest furniture store in town. It spent hundreds of thousands of dollars advertising in the local newspaper. I knew this was going to be a challenge.

My first call was on the store owner, who referred me to his advertising agency when I called to get an appointment. I went there once just to say I had, then called the owner for another appointment, laying the idea pitch on him as thickly as I could. He must have sensed I wasn't going away, so he agreed to give me 15 minutes.

That first call was a textbook Creative Selling System presentation, although I didn't know that at the time—I was just following my instincts. The owner didn't say much until I asked for the order, which was for $60,000, or 60 times the amount he had spent with us before.

He didn't blink at the amount, but he told me that he didn't like the idea, so he wasn't going to buy it. I asked him if I could come back with another idea, and he said something that created a selling monster. He said I was always welcome *as long as I brought him a new idea* to consider. "You never know," he said. "Someday you just might hit one."

He didn't know my mother, so I'm sure he didn't know how stubborn I can be. I adopted a very simple game plan: I would pitch him a different idea every week until he bought one of them or until one of us died. I kept the same dollar proposal and developed, borrowed, or otherwise created a new idea for him every week.

That went on for exactly 52 weeks. I didn't want to lose my rhythm, so I even made that weekly call while I was on vacation that year. While I was waiting to see him each week, I met everyone in the store. I was there so often, I learned the names of most of his customers. I became a semiexpert in the furniture business by osmosis. Every week he gave me my 15 minutes and ended them by saying no.

The biggest problem I had, of course, was the number of ideas I used. I couldn't pitch the same thing twice, so I needed a new one every week. The station copywriters and commercial producers hid from me. The sales manager refused to let me nominate furniture stores for our weekly brainstorming session. But somehow the ideas came—one every single week.

One day, one of the commercial producers collared me and said he had something to show me. We went back to the master control room, where he loaded a piece of videotape on one of the machines. "I was fooling around last night and this happened," he said. "Watch this monitor." He rolled the tape and I saw the furniture store's logo, which appeared with an electronically generated moving tail like a comet's. By today's standards it would be primitive, but back in those dark ages of TV, it was unique. The tape lasted 4 seconds.

I called the store owner and asked him to come to the station to see something. This was in the days before portable videocassette players. When he saw the logo with the comet's tail, he said just two words: "That's it."

I got the order after 52 presentations—the last one based on a 4-second idea. That contract made the furniture store the station's largest advertiser that year. My commissions on the account enabled my wife and I to buy our first home. Stubborn? Yes, and proud of it.

On reflection, my biggest reward from that sale was the lesson I learned about the power of selling an idea. The decision maker never would have seen me twice, let alone 52 times, if I hadn't brought him an idea at the beginning and another one on each successive call.

Creative selling celebrates the relationship between buyers and sellers. You know your idea is a success when buyers' eyes light up as you explain it,

> Just like anything else in life that promises great rewards, creative selling takes dedication.

when they start making suggestions to modify it to even better meet their needs, when they say yes and give you the order. Until it's sold, the idea only exists in your mind and on paper. But when the buyer says yes, the idea comes to life. The two of you have created something together.

Just like anything else in life that promises great rewards, creative selling takes dedication. You've already demonstrated a great deal of dedication to your art by slogging through this book and enduring my circumlocutions, rants and war stories. I hope you take the lessons to heart and use the Creative Selling System to achieve your own rewards.

# INDEX

## A

Account priorities
  active, 195–197
  activity priorities and, 200
  new, 197–199
Activity priorities, 199–201
*American Demographics,*
  17, 23
Appearance, 76
Appointments
  length of, 65
  making, 60–70
Attitude
  negative vs. positive, 107
  during negotiations, 150
  toward objections, 106

## B

Ben Franklin close, 143
BFO (best-and-final offer), 154
Body language, 77–78
Brainstorming, 23–28, 34–35
Business cards, 176
Buying agencies, 166, 168, 169

## C

Call reports, 205–206
Canvassing
  category, 173–174
  cold, 172–173
Census information, 16, 20–21
Clients. *See* Customers
Closed doors

opening with persistence,
  68–70
opening with videotape
  presentation, 97–103
Closing
  fear of, 131
  head-nodding, 132
  myths about, 129–131
  overcoming delays, 141–144
  persistence and, 134–135
  techniques, 135–141,
    143–144
  timing, 132–135
  trial, 134
  words to avoid in, 138
Cold-calls. *See also* Canvassing
  dropping in, 59–60
  making appointments, 60–70
  persistence in, 68–70
  recipe for, 60
  rehearsing, 66–67
Columbo close, 143
Communications skills, 71–73.
  *See also* Listening
Competitors
  impact of, 3–4, 15
  monitoring, 177
  prospects', 25
Complex sales, 159–169
  closing, 130–131
  decision influencers and,
    160–162, 164
  decision process in,
    162–166

# ABOUT
# THE AUTHOR

**D**ave Donelson is President of Sales Development Associates, a consulting firm he founded in 1988. The author's 30-plus years of experience in sales and consulting makes him an invaluable source for any reader looking to start (or jumpstart) a sales career. By training salespeople to sell ideas instead of products, Mr. Donelson has helped increase sales by 20 percent or more for a wide range of companies.

The author's resume includes clients in heavy manufacturing, construction, cable, radio and television broadcasting, magazine publishing, industrial sales, retailing, and consumer services. He has also started up three companies himself.

Mr. Donelson's latest undertaking is the Enterprise Learning Center, an Internet-based training delivery service offering online versions of SDA's training programs as well as those of other firms.

Mr. Donelson lives in West Harrsion, New York, with his wife, Nora. He can be contacted at davedonelson@elconline.com or at (914) 949-7483.

# ABOUT
# ENTREPRENEUR

**E**ntrepreneur Media Inc., founded in 1973, is the nation's leading authority on small and entrepreneurial businesses.

Anchored by *Entrepreneur* magazine, which is read by more than 2 million people monthly, Entrepreneur Media boasts a stable of magazines, including *Entrepreneur's Start-ups*, *Entrepreneur's Be Your Own Boss*, *Entrepreneur's Home Office* e-zine, *Franchise Zone* e-zine, and *Entrepreneur Mexico*.

But Entrepreneur Media is more than just magazines. Entrepreneur.com is the world's largest Web site devoted to small business and features smallbizsearch.com, a search engine targeting small-business topics.

Entrepreneur Press, started in 1998, publishes books to inspire and inform readers. For information about a customized version of this book, contact Christie Barnes Stafford at (949) 261-2325 or e-mail her at cstafford@entrepreneurmag.com.

CURRENT TITLES FROM ENTREPRENEUR PRESS:

*Benjamin Franklin's 12 Rules Of Management:*
*The Founding Father of American Business Solves Your Toughest Problems*

*Business Plans Made Easy:*
*It's Not as Hard as You Think*

*Financial Fitness in 45 Days:*
*The Complete Guide to Shaping Up Your Finances*

*Get Smart:*
*365 Tips to Boost Your Entrepreneurial IQ*

*Knock-Out Marketing:*
*Powerful Strategies to Punch Up Your Sales*

*Radicals & Visionaries:*
*Entrepreneurs Who Revolutionized the 20th Century*

*Start Your Own Business:*
*The Only Start-up Book You'll Ever Need*

*Success for Less:*
*100 Low-Cost Businesses You Can Start Today*

*303 Marketing Tips Guaranteed to Boost Your Business*

*Young Millionaires:*
*Inspiring Stories to Ignite Your Entrepreneurial Dreams*

*Where's The Money?*
*Sure-Fire Financial Solutions for Your Small Business*


FORTHCOMING TITLES FROM ENTREPRENEUR PRESS:

*How to be a Teenage Millionaire:*
*Start Your Own Business, Make Your Own Money and Run Your Own Life*

*Extreme Investor:*
*Intelligent Information From the Edge*

*How to Dotcom:*
*A Step-by-Step Guide to E-Commerce*

*Grow Your Business*

# The Secrets and Lives of the 20th Century's Most Influential Innovators and Trailblazers

The 20th Century marked an era of unprecedented progress, growth and ingenuity. *RADICALS AND VISIONARIES* reveals the complete stories of over 70 legendary masters of enterprise and the unsung entrepreneurial heroes who charted the course of business throughout the century. You'll discover little-known facts and learn the success secrets of such movers and shakers as:

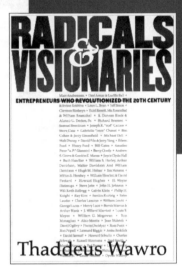

- *Former cabaret singer Coco Chanel who thumbed her nose at the suffocating styles of the 19th century and sparked a fashion revolution that still influences designers today*

- *Ron Popeil, a part-time carnival huckster and cutlery salesman whose late-night TV commercials for kitchen gadgets kicked off the infomercial phenomenon*

- *A.P. Giannini, the greengrocer with no financial experience who took on "the suits" and founded the world's largest bank*

RADICALS & VISIONARIES is a lively, revealing, and often astonishing chronicle of the lives and accomplishments of the most influential entrepreneurs of the past 100 years.

ISBN 1-891984-13-6    $17.95    paperback    460 pages    72 b & w photos    (Price subject to change)

Available at **www.smallbizbooks.com** and at local and online bookstores

Entrepreneur Press

# "Mandatory reading for any small-business owner who is serious about success."

— *Jay Conrad Levinson,*
*author, Guerrilla Marketing*
*series of books*

## Powerhouse Marketing Tactics for Making Big Profits

Written for both new and established small-business owners, this nuts-and-bolts guide gives you the marketing firepower you need to satisfy customers, attract prospects, boost your profits and blast the competition.

Packed with proven techniques, tips and advice, this easy-to-read guide covers every aspect of marketing, including:

- How to think like a marketer
- How to select the best markets for your products and services
- 4 common marketing mistakes and how to avoid them
- Tips for writing your marketing plan
- Sure-fire selling tactics that get results
- Building your presence on the internet

ISBN 1-891984-04-7
$19.95
paperback
296 pages
(price subject to change)

Available at **www.smallbizbooks.com** and at local and online bookstores

**Entrepreneur Press**

# Start a Revolution in Your Management Thinking!

**Explore the innovative management principles and philosophies of a man many consider the "Founding Father of American Business" including:**

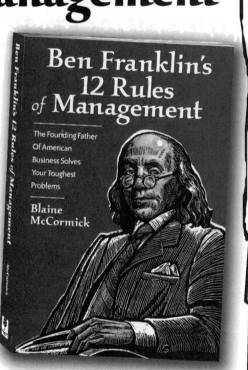

- Great managers rarely have great beginnings

- Seek first to manage yourself, then to manage others

- Influence is more important than victory

- Become a revolutionary for positive experimentation and change

- Sometimes it's better to do 1,001 small things right than one large thing right

## Please visit smallbizbooks.com for more information or to order

**$14.95 PAPERBACK  240 PAGES**

# A NO PAIN, ALL GAIN

## WORKOUT FOR BUILDING YOUR MONETARY MUSCLE!

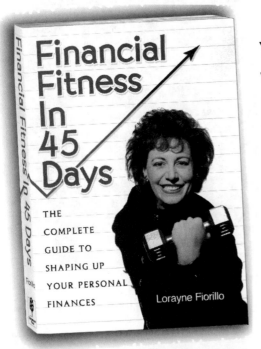

Your workout starts with a six-day warm-up aimed at revealing problem areas. After a 36-day, step-by-step financial workout, you end with a three-day cool down designed to maintain your long-term financial fitness.

An easy-to-follow one-exercise-a-day program, FINANCIAL FITNESS IN 45 DAYS will help you crunch the investment numbers and whip your portfolio into shape.

### Please visit **smallbizbooks.com**
### for more information or to order

$19.95 PAPERBACK          375 PAGES

# Stop

## Dreaming

## And start your own business today.

**Start-Up Success Set**

First choose from 100 low-cost, in-demand businesses listed in Success For Less. We have also included 25 inexpensive businesses you can start and run on a part-time basis, on weekends, in the evenings or whenever you've got a few free hours to earn extra income.

Then let Starting Your Own Business help you step-by-step through the process of starting your own business. Written in a friendly, down-to-earth style, Starting Your Own Business makes it easy to understand even the most complex business issues so you can reach your goals and enjoy the rewards of owning your own business.

Call and order your Start-Up Success Set today.

**Item #2020**

## Start-Up Success Set
### for only $50
Regular price $83.95

### Order Toll Free
## 1-800-421-2300
### 24 hours a day

Source code **DLIN**

**Entrepreneur** MAGAZINE

SMALL BUSINESS RESOURCE CATALOG
P.O. BOX 432, NEWBURGH, NY 12551

# 50 ways to make your business dreams come true!

Yes! You can make your dreams come true. We'll show you how.

For over 20 years our Business Start-Up Guides have helped people just like you start and run their own successful businesses.

These step-by-step how-to guides teach you everything you need to plan, run and grow your business. And with over 50 different guides to choose from, you're sure to find the business of your dreams.

Call for your FREE catalog today.

## Inside each Start-up Guide you'll find—

- Business Plans
- Market Location
- Record Keeping & Taxes
- Advertising & Promotions

- Accounting & Start-up Costs
- Equipment & Inventory
- Financing
- Government Help

### Here is a sample of some of the guides we have available:

1817 Apparel Business
1813 Bringing Your Product to Market
1151 Consulting
1800 Creating a Successful Business Plan
1313 Event Planning Services

1806 Financing Your Small Business
1400 Food Service
1306 Gift Basket Service
1092 Import/Export Business
1393 Internet Entrepreneur
1015 Mail-Order Business

1812 Managing Your Small Business
1345 Medical Claims Processing
1815 Starting & Running a Homebased Business
1811 Starting Your Own Business

## CALL TOLL FREE

# 1·800·421·2300

### AND USE SOURCE CODE DLMN

## Entrepreneur MAGAZINE
SMALL BUSINESS RESOURCE CATALOG
P.O. Box 432 Newburgh, NY 12551

## Visit our website at smallbizbooks.com

# Get in the Know!

Please enter my subscription to *Entrepreneur's Start-Ups* for one year. I will receive 12 issues for only $11.97. That's a savings of 66% off the newsstand price. The free issue is mine to keep, even if I choose not to subscribe.

Name ☐ Mr. ☐ Mrs._____
(please print)

Address_____

City_____ State_____ Zip _____

[ ] BILL ME [ ] PAYMENT ENCLOSED

**Guaranteed. Or your money back.** Every subscription to Entrepreneur's Start-Ups comes with a 100% satisfaction guarantee: your money back whenever you like, for whatever reason, on all unmailed issues! Offer good in U.S. and possessions only. Please allow 4–6 weeks for mailing of first issue. Canadian and foreign: $34.97. U.S. funds only.

5HBR7

**MAIL THIS COUPON TO:**
Entrepreneur's Start-Ups
P.O. Box 50368
Boulder, CO 80321-0368

**Entrepreneur's Start•Ups**

## Plus a FREE issue + SAVE 66%

# Million Dollar Secrets

Exercise your right to make it **BIG**. Get into the small business authority—now at **75% OFF** the newsstand price!

**YES!** Start my 1 year subscription and bill me for just $11.97. I get a full year of *Entrepreneur* and save 75% off the newsstand rate. If I choose not to subscribe, the free issue is mine to keep.

Name ☐ Mr. ☐ Mrs._____
(please print)

Address _____

City_____ State _____ Zip _____

[ ] BILL ME [ ] PAYMENT ENCLOSED

5G8K8

**Guaranteed. Or your money back.** Every subscription to Entrepreneur comes with a 100% satisfaction guarantee: your money back whenever you like, for whatever reason, on all unmailed issues! Offer good in U.S. and possessions only. Please allow 4–6 weeks for mailing of first issue. Canadian and foreign: $39.97. U.S. funds only.

Plus a FREE issue!

**MAIL THIS COUPON TO:**

**Entrepreneur MAGAZINE**
P.O. Box 50368
Boulder, CO 80321-0368